The Congregation as Church

The Congregation as Church

Kenneth A. Kuntz

THE BETHANY PRESS
ST. LOUIS, MISSOURI

Library of Congress Catalog Card Number: 70-168892

ISBN: 0-8272-0434-5

Artwork for charts on pages 79, 83, 84, 85, 86, and 87 by Florence Dodson

Distributed by the G. R. Welch Company, Toronto, Ontario, Canada.

MANUFACTURED IN THE UNITED STATES OF AMERICA

Foreword

A comprehensive reassessment of the nature, function, and organization of the local congregation is needed today. The dynamic changes that have taken place in all the structures of society, including churches, call for this. New theological insights into the nature of the church and its mission in the world provide new understandings of ecclesiastical organization and new insights into the meaning of obedience to the gospel in relationship to human needs. Experience gained in recent decades as well as the critical attention given to problems of congregational structure and program make such a reassessment urgent.

Congregations related to the Christian Church (Disciples of Christ) now stand in a challenging, new relationship to the whole church of which they are a part. This relationship is set forth in the Provisional Design for the Christian Church (Disciples of Christ), which recognizes three basic manifestations of church—congregational, regional, and general. These are united within one body by a common covenant. Each manifestation at the level for which it is uniquely equipped to serve is characterized by its integrity, self-government, authority, rights and responsibilities. Representative government establishes the channels of communication and provides for meaningful interdependence.

Not since the publication of *The Church Functioning Effectively* by O. L. Shelton in 1946 has there been an attempt to examine congregational life and work among the Disciples of Christ in depth.

The Congregation as Church is such a book. While it seeks to conserve the best out of past experience, it is not a mere rehashing of old concepts. It takes a fresh, new approach to the congregation. It will give insight, motivation, and guidance and serve to meet the congregation's need to discover what God wants it to do in the modern world. It will also provide practical guidelines for developing the ways and means by which the church orders its life in order to fulfill its mission of witness and service to mankind today.

Dr. Kuntz is eminently qualified to make this reassessment of the congregation as church. For over twenty years he was a highly successful pastor, serving for seven years at the First Christian Church in Chillicothe, Missouri, and sixteen years at First Christian Church, Hannibal. As a leader in the regional organization of the Christian Church in Missouri, he played a key role in guiding the state organizations into unification. Now as the executive chairman of the Division of Homeland Ministries (U.C.M.S.) of the Christian Church (Disciples of Christ), he carries broad administrative responsibilities for creative work in areas of church development.

Dr. Kuntz understands the dynamics of the present world situation and its impact upon structure and function and the need for wholeness. He realizes the need for flexibility and diversity in the forms and functions of congregational life. He also recognizes the importance of down-to-earth, manageable guidelines for congregational development.

I believe this book, radiant with faith in the church, realistic about its need for reformation and renewal, confident of the constructive role it has to play in the future, will be of great help to ministers, church members, and congregations as they prepare to move forward into the 1970s.

A. Dale Fiers
General Minister and President
Christian Church (Disciples of Christ)

Preface

Congregations of all Christian denominations are caught today in the dilemma of choosing between the inflexibility of institutionalism and the free-wheeling and revolutionary forces sometimes called *renewal*. This uncertainty challenges the organization of the church and prompts consideration of new styles of life and work in the congregation.

These new styles of life and work will not be dictated by activities designed to keep the *form* of the church alive. Congregational self-interest is not acceptable. It never was. The congregation must turn itself outward to God as revealed through Jesus Christ in the world.

Consequently, some of the reasons for writing this book are as follows:

- To aid the congregation in discovering what God wants it to do
- To aid the congregation in discovering the kind of world in which it lives
- To aid the congregation in developing a style of life and work that appropriately engages the individual member and the corporate congregation in a servant role in the world

Obviously the task is too great to be treated in any single book. It is hoped, however, that these pages will open new vistas of thought and make possible congregational development of new styles of life and work.

Many have shared their counsel in the preparation of this book. It is impossible to recognize all who have assisted other than by categories. Regional executive ministers, general church officers and staff, professors of seminaries and undergraduate institutions of higher education, ministers and lay leaders have given their advice and counsel to the author.

This opportunity is taken to express personal gratitude and appreciation to all who have so ably assisted in this important venture. They have, without necessarily subscribing to the ideas set forth, individually and collectively helped to shape this book.

Contents

PART I

The Christian Church

1

God's Mission

God is alive! He is the God of history—past, present, and future. He is the God of Abraham, Isaac, and Jacob; of Jonas Salk, Martin Luther King, Jr., and Dietrich Bonhoeffer. He is your God and mine. He is a God with a mission.

God's mission is declared by Paul, writing to the congregation at Corinth: " ... God was in Christ reconciling the world to himself, ... and entrusting to us the message of reconciliation" (2 Cor. 5:19). God's mission may be identified in the reconciling and redemptive action of love revealed in the life of Jesus Christ. God's mission is directed to man and his human situation.

God's mission is evident in his justice, which cascades upon our human situation. He deals with justice that expresses itself in judgment and, through the process of judgment, opens the way to hope. Jeremiah declares, "Behold, the days are coming, says the Lord, when I will raise up for David a righteous Branch, and he shall reign as king and deal wisely, and shall execute justice and righteousness in the land" (23:5).

God's judgment is working in the world. The tragic era of man's history following 1918 and the Allied victory in Europe bears testimony to a world insensitive to the terrible need of people starving in Germany. The seeds of destruction were sown in the awful soil of human privation and sprouted the evil growth of Adolf Hitler. The holocaust of 1939–45 was the result—a judgment of God on a world insensitive to the depth of human want. The same insensitivity in the world has allowed three hundred years of maltreatment of the American Indian and Negro and has brought God's judgment upon the church and the government of the United States of America in the form of riots, demands, and the beginning of a more integrated life-style.

God is hope, also! There is hope in God's love as it reconciles man to man. The redemptive power of God's love made evident through human deeds may be seen breaking out all around the world. The World Council of Churches meeting in Uppsala, Sweden (1968), was confronted with the needs of the Biafran hungry. Spearheaded by German and other European churches, a program of Biafran relief was instituted.

Another sign of God's love is found in the United States, where youth, as well as their elders, are engaged in a variety of peace movements. In conjunction with this is another sign, although seen dimly: the decreased use of war as an option for settling human disagreements and conflicts. The love of God is symbolized by the resurrection of Christ and his leading of the church to a ministry of redemption and reconciliation upon earth. Surely this prayer will be fulfilled:

> Thy kingdom come,
> Thy will be done,
> On earth as it is in heaven.
> —Matthew 6:10

You ask, What has all this to do with the church? Just this! The church accepts God as a God of history. But it must do more. It must constantly seek to discover what God is doing in the world. *A Plan of Union,* prepared by the Consultation on Church Union, puts it this way: "Faithfulness to the Gospel through mission in the world shall be the primary characteristic of the church's life at every level." And again this hard fact is evident: the church must discover what God is doing and respond to his mission.

The church has long been committed to mission, but too often the mission has become *missions*. The result has been the emergence of "foreign missions," "home missions," and specific geographical locations of mission enterprises on a world map. Such institutionalization of *mission* has tended to make each enterprise a project in isolation and has reduced the work accomplished to projects expressed in "doing deeds of kindness."

The present day calls for the church to touch the nerve center of God's mission. The church is required to discover anew and constantly what *God* is doing. It is imperative that the church discover what God wants done and get on with the work. It is for each Christian and the church to be used by God, to become his servant people in the world.

Awareness of God's mission has come fairly recently to the life of the church in renewed form. It was Emil Brunner who said, "The church exists by mission as a fire exists by burning." The World Council of Churches meeting in New Delhi (1961) brought to life the latent concern for understanding and activating God's mission. Subsequently, study groups were formed in Europe and North America. An increasing flow of books, articles, and denominational studies has motivated renewal groups of various kinds. The church is today beginning with renewed vigor to take seriously God's mission.

Mission is a word not clearly understood, yet widely used. Newspapers, radio, and television use the well-known phrase, "This is mission control." The military conducts an action against the enemy and reports, "Mission accomplished." The United States sends a "cultural mission" to Russia.

The world *mission* is used also in the church. An old definition of it is the "act or an instance of sending." The mission of the church is to accept its "sentness" in the world and respond to God's ministry of reconciliation. This definition, combined with new understandings of purpose, perspective, and action, properly relates mission to God and the church.

Mission Purpose

Purpose in mission deals with response to, and the living out of, God's love for the whole world. It is the involvement in what Paul called the "ministry of reconciliation" (2 Cor. 5:18).

Purpose in mission deals with spiritual renewal. John C. Bennett, past president of Union Theological Seminary, New York, is reported by the press to have said:

> A stripped-down, relevant version of Christianity may be effective for the moment in dealing with a particular problem. But it ... fails to mediate the grace of forgiveness and of new life that the whole person needs, and it knows little of the sources of reconciliation that society requires for its healing.

Spiritual renewal may be derived from several sources, one of which is deep study of the Scriptures and of theology. It is also the result of wrestling in prayer with what John Macquarrie has called "a pathological disorder in human life, a radical alienation deep within our existence...."[1] The

1. *Studies in Christian Existentialism* (Philadelphia: Westminster Press, 1965), p. 7.

reality of sin has to be dealt with in mission. It has to be dealt with simultaneously with the issues of human need. Spiritual renewal must undergird and strengthen human renewal.

Purpose in mission deals with sharing the "good news" with all people, which includes the meeting of human need. The danger is that mission may become more interested in institutionalizing its response than with the content of its response. Manifestly the content will likely be expressed in some institutional form, but the form must always be flexible and able to change. For example, education that frees man from ignorance is of greater importance than the building where learning takes place, and healing that frees man from disease is of greater importance than a hospital building.

Mission Perspective

Mission for the church is strengthened with the *perspective* of one world. According to Genesis, God created one world; and in the Gospel According to John we read, "For God so loved the world that he gave his only Son, that whoever believes in him should not perish but have eternal life" (3:16). Paul, writing to the Ephesians, identifies Christ's reconciling ministry which makes possible the constant unfolding of one world: "And he came and preached peace to you who were far off and peace to those who were near; for through him we both have access in one Spirit to the Father. So then you are no longer strangers and sojourners, but you are fellow citizens with the saints and members of the household of God" (2:17–19).

The perspective of one world makes the meaning of races, ethnic groups, and nations of secondary importance. Paul declares in his sermon on Mars Hill, "He made from one every nation of men to live on all the face of the earth ..."

(Acts 17:26). Again, it was Paul, writing to the Galatians, who said, "There is neither Jew nor Greek, there is neither slave nor free, there is neither male nor female; for you are all one in Christ Jesus" (3:28).

Mission has a world view of man and his condition, and man in his relationship with God. For those living within the United States, this means accepting the fact that the North American continent—all of it—is only one of the seven continents involved in mission. Such a perspective means that each congregation must be engaged in mission in its own community and in the whole world.

Perspective in mission deals with issues that are common to man in one world. Issues such as love, sin, guilt, forgiveness, and the discovery of human purpose are as essentially a part of mission as are justice, war, peace, poverty, and affluence. Each issue may have various degrees of intensity in different areas of the world. Malnutrition, for instance, may be part of the poverty issue in the United States, while starvation may be part of the same issue in Asia, Africa, and South America. The church must relieve such intense human suffering, wherever it may be.

Mission Action

Action in mission means releasing the love of God in the whole world. It means understanding that all men are embraced in God's concern. In sweeping terms, it is possible to say that God's task is stated in the words of Christ: "For the Son of man came to seek and to save the lost" (Luke 19:10). Such a generic statement must be refined by reading the study of judgment found in Matthew, which declares, "Truly, I say to you, as you did it to one of the least of these my brethren, you did it to me" (25:40). The "least of these" includes you and me, the next-door neighbor, and the faceless and nameless persons halfway around the world. It includes the poor and the affluent, the inner-city and the suburban dweller, the black, the brown, the red, the yellow, and the white.

True *action* in mission means sharing love, abilities, and resources without questioning the worthiness of the recipient. Jesus, as recorded by Matthew in the Sermon on the Mount, expressed it this way: "... for he makes his sun rise on the evil and on the good, and sends rain on the just and on the unjust" (5:45).

Summary

God is at work in our world, and he is calling his church to share in his mission. But we must discover God's mission in *our time and place, then act upon the meaning of that discovery.*

The church—individual Christian and congregation—is "sent" in terms of the Great Commission: "Go therefore and make disciples of all nations ..." (Matt. 28:19). The Gospel According to John records Jesus as saying, "... As the Father has sent me, even so I send you" (20:21). Paul, interpreting the commission, summed up the matter succinctly in the thirteenth chapter of 1 Corinthians: "If I speak in the tongues of men and of angels, but have not love, I am a noisy gong or a clanging cymbal.... So faith, hope, love abide, these three; but the greatest of these is love" (vv. 1, 13).

2

The World

There is one God! God created the world, and he created men to live together in this one world.

The story of creation in Genesis tells us, "So God created man in his own image, in the image of God he created him; male and female he created them" (1:27). Whatever else "in his own image" means, one generally accepted meaning is that God created man free to make choices. However, from the Garden of Eden story to the crucifixion of our Lord, the freedom of man is accompanied with responsibility for choices made. This is the awful burden and great opportunity of every individual.

Man has sought to shoulder his burden in two basic ways. The first was the development of rigid systems of human conduct established by code and law and administered by superiors. The result of such a system for the individual is evidenced in the book *Thoughts of the Servant of God:* "From what anxieties do we not free ourselves by making the vow of obedience! How happy are single-minded religious. Their sole guide being the will of Superiors, they are ever secure of going the right way without fear of error, should it even appear to them certain that the Superiors are mistaken."[1] The authority of superiors and the obedience of followers made making choices the responsibility of the superiors and acceptance the task of the followers. This kind of thinking caused the development of monolithic structures in governments of state and provided the framework for a seemingly safe and secure society for centuries.

The second way man has attempted to bear the burden of responsibility for choices made is by personal responsibility in an open and free society. The university movement of the Renaissance (fourteenth through sixteenth centuries) set the stage for renewal of the class influences in life. Centers of learning began to take form and men began to ask questions not critically studied since the fall of Rome (fifth century). Scientific discoveries of this period of history were made by Copernicus (1473–1543), Galileo (1564–1642), and Harvey (1578-1657); and these discoveries raised questions regarding man and his world.

In more recent times Charles Darwin's theory of evolution and Pierre Teilhard de Chardin's use of the theory of evolution in the development of theology,[2] together with the work of Dietrich Bonhoeffer,[3] have served to awaken man and his life and structure in the church to the meaning of personal and corporate responsibility of choice-making. In addition, Bishop Robinson's *Honest to God,* Harvey Cox's *The Secular City,* and Ronald Gregor Smith's *Secular Christianity* have served to open further the channels of both the world and the church to the meaning of responsibility in freedom. Finally, the great issues of the world in these fading

1. Saint Thérèse of the Child Jesus, *Thoughts of the Servant of God* (New York: P. J. Kenedy & Sons, 1915), p. 95.

2. *The Phenomenon of Man,* trans. Bernard Wall (New York: Harper & Row, Harper Torchbooks, 1961).

3. *The Cost of Discipleship,* trans. R. H. Fuller, rev. and unabr. ed. (New York: Macmillan Co., 1959).

years of the twentieth century are showing man that there is no safe, secure place in systems and structures. Swelling world populations and rampant poverty make it impossible to follow in assumed safety and security.

The two ways of handling freedom—rigid systems or personal responsibility in an open and free society—are in sharp conflict in our day. But it seems clear that the latter has the momentum of the hour and very possibly history on its side.

Acceptance of the world as God's world and man as God's creation with the attributes of freedom and responsibility for his choices, makes it necessary for man to understand the world and his relationship to it.

Charles Dickens wrote about his world, "It was the best of times and the worst of times." Recently, Barbara Ward, of England, said of our times, "Never has so much wealth produced so little welfare." God's one world is severely divided between the affluent and the poor, the white and the nonwhite, the uneducated and the learned.

A variety of issues forms the substance of this division. Man has the opportunity to choose justice or injustice, humane treatment or inhumane treatment of his fellowman, peace or war. He is responsible for all his choices. This responsibility makes it necessary for him to view himself, the world, and all human life in their wholeness. As Barbara Ward has pointed out, "we need a planetary view" of our world and of man's life in the world.

In a planetary view of the world, the issues of justice, war, and peace, for example, are both personal and corporate. They are issues that transcend national and hemispheric boundaries; they include the whole of human life.

Many elements make for justice or militate against it. One of these is economics. Most of the world's monetary, industrial, and agricultural wealth is in the hands of those living in only a few countries of the world. These are the affluent, having average yearly family incomes upward of $7,000. The average yearly income of the remaining families in the world is $1,500, with half of these families receiving less than $500 per year.

One of the problems facing man is how to share the monetary, industrial, and agricultural wealth of the affluent nations with those in poverty. Aside from the problems of governmental procedures and the means of transportation of food between the affluent and poor peoples of the world is the basic question of motivation. Do we earnestly desire to share our wealth and the means of making wealth under the mandate of the gospel of Jesus Christ? The answer is not clear when the United States is presently giving only about one-half of 1 percent of its gross national product to serve the poor in the world—and this when the gross national product increases about 5 percent per year. Add to this the fact that the average church member in the United States gives approximately one-half of 1 percent of his total church giving for overseas mission work. Yet, before all Christians stand the ancient words, "for I was *hungry* and you gave me food, I was *thirsty* and you gave me drink, I was a *stranger* and you welcomed me, I was *naked* and you clothed me, I was *sick* and you visited me, I was in *prison* and you came to me" (Matt. 23:35–36, italics added).

Man chooses what he will do, and he is responsible for his choices. Man may choose to feed or not to feed, clothe or not to clothe, shelter or not to shelter those in need. But if he refuses to meet human need, he must share in the suffering and shame of those living in poverty. Justice, among other things, calls for understanding a world in which the majority of people are poor and alleviation of their poverty is a prime matter.

Every human being has the right to fulfill his human potential limited only by his ambition. For example, everyone has the right to live out the years of his life to their full unhindered by man's inhumane treatment. The average life expectancy of a citizen of the United States is a little more than seventy years. The average life expectancy of a migrant worker in this nation is approximately forty-five years. Why is there this difference of twenty-five years? The difference is the result of diet, housing, working conditions, and many other factors. Many migrant workers put food on the tables in American homes at the awful price of suffering themselves from malnutrition, inadequate housing, and substandard sanitary conditions. The life of the migrant worker is an illustration in cameo of the condition of life for most of the world's population. The basic question is, How can the Christian help to overcome the hiatus between the poor and the affluent of the world? The ancient question "Am I my brother's keeper?" (Gen. 4:9) still stands unanswered in deed. For the Christian, the answer should be clear. The Scriptures, beginning with the story of Cain and Abel and including the parable of the Good Samaritan, are definite on this point.

The search for world peace is one of the great issues of mankind. Peace is not to be understood as "being at rest" but as living life in that delicate tension which provides meaning for life. Peace is the product of love and trust. It seeks to build upon those qualities of life which see beyond the immediate positions and deeds of men and nations to what can be.

Peace has been the dream of man in every age. Isaiah observed:

> He [the Lord] shall judge between the nations,
> and shall decide for many peoples;
> and they shall beat their swords into plowshares,
> and their spears into pruning hooks;
> nation shall not lift up sword against nation,
> neither shall they learn war any more.
>
> —Isaiah 2:4

The Christ said, "... my peace I give to you ..." (John 14:27). A new breed of peacemakers is in our world today. It appears that many of the youth are the new peacemakers and they are putting into action what the world has dreamed about and what the church has taught for centuries. The youth are saying, "We will not go to war." Instead, they want to direct their lives toward serving all men on this planet in the struggle against poverty and injustice. The youth want to make it possible to have a world of justice where each individual can develop to his full humanity.

Impractical as the actions of some of the youth may seem to be, the fact remains that they are causing the positions of governments to change and to extend their search for peace. Many of the youth are taking seriously the teachings of the church and making real the witness of the Christ who bore crucifixion rather than attempt to usher in the kingdom of God by the power of the sword.

Summary

The world is God's. Man in God's world has many needs, among them the need for justice, well-being, and peace. The church has both the opportunity and the responsibility to aid man in making viable choices to meet his human situation, because it has been entrusted with the gospel of Jesus Christ. Man will make critical choices in a free society as he seeks to strengthen the development of justice, peace, and well-being for all men. Consequently, his task is to make evident the love of God for all persons in the whole world.

3

The Church

God works in the world through his church.

The church is sometimes described as the people who are "called out." This is based on an understanding of the Greek word *ekklesia,* translated "church" in the New Testament (cf. Matt. 16:18; 18:17; also references in the Acts of the Apostles and some of the epistles). However, "church" has come to have a variety of meanings. Three essential meanings are evident today.

First, the church is understood by some to be concerned with the salvation of the individual and only secondarily, if at all, concerned or responsible for the world around that individual. The focus is on the eternal or otherworldly life. This interpretation is reflected in the monastic movement and certain so-called fundamentalist groups.

Second, the church is interpreted as being primarily concerned with responding to human need by, for example, feeding the hungry, clothing the naked, sheltering the homeless, and engaging in social-action activities such as community projects and legislation. This interpretation sees salvation as that which is expressed in *doing here and now* with little if any focus on the otherworldly.

Third, for many people, the church is understood as a fellowship of faith and worship designed to provide opportunity for individual and group spiritual renewal and action. These people see the church as being a part of this world, yet not of this world. They see this world as being under the purposes and judgment of God, but they are committed to responding to God's mission as expressed in this world. Consequently, these individuals can respond to God's mission in this world and feel they are prepared to respond to whatever world lies beyond.

The "called out" respond to God's mission to partake of and participate in a special fellowship or *koinonia*. The New Testament *koinonia* means "fellowship." (See Acts 2:42; 1 Cor. 1:9; 2 Cor. 8:4, KJV.) It also means "partnership" and "partners." (See 2 Cor. 6:14; 1 Cor. 10:20.)

It is appropriate, therefore, to refer to the church as that special fellowship in which there is a common commitment to one another—and to God revealed through Jesus Christ—as partners in God's mission.

Since God's mission is to the world, the church is not to be understood in terms of structure or geography. It is to be understood in terms of mission within God's mission. The church may be anyplace. It cuts across all social, economic, and other lines of distinction. This understanding of the church is distressing to those who want neat definitions of membership, structure, and geography.

Certain facts are becoming increasingly clear to contemporary church life. Having one's name on the roll in a congregation does not mean that an individual is a part of God's church. Membership in the fellowship (koinonia) can mean that the individual has the opportunity of being a partaker in God's mission. Partaking in God's mission has two basic areas of responsibility: first, responsibility to the fellowship; and, second, responsibility to the world. The individual, however, often fails to see that membership in the fellowship affects more than his personal life. The result is the development of a personal piety divorced from corporate action and unrelated to the human situation. Personal piety, although generally content with individual achievement of the "good life," is sometimes involved in meeting human need on a person-to-person basis.

Specific deeds of Christian action are generally manifested by those who take God's mission seriously and are committed to personal and corporate response to that mission. They recognize the importance of personal religious development and, at the same time, are involved in effective response to God's mission through deeds in the life of the church and in the world.

The combination of individual commitment and corporate action allows the opportunity for personal, congregational, and ecumenical expressions of mission. It is important to note that congregations can join with other congregations in community or conciliar action at the city, state, national, or world level to engage in mission action. In this connection there are three essential categories in God's mission, namely, nurture of the fellowship, witness in the community, and witness in the world.

Nurture of the Fellowship

The Christian has an obligation to express in deed his concern for the nurture of the fellowship. The quality of life of the fellowship is essentially a matter of nurture made evident in effective action in mission.

The nurture of the fellowship is a practical or applied way of life based on Christians' love for one another within the fellowship. Jesus' relationship with the disciples was one of love. He put it this way: "No longer do I call you servants, for the servant does not know what his master is doing; but I have called you friends, for all that I have heard from my Father I have made known to you. You did not choose me, but I chose you and appointed you that you should go and bear fruit and that your fruit should abide; so that whatever you ask the Father in my name, he may give it to you. This I command you, to love one another" (John 15:15–17).

Manifestly, the quality of the life of the fellowship is important as the foundation from which both the individual and the corporate expressions of the church move into the world to participate in God's mission. However, it is not sufficient to be concerned only with the well-being of the fellowship; common identity, or oneness, with those beyond the immediate fellowship is also important. Christ said: "While he was still speaking to the people, behold, his mother and his brothers stood outside, asking to speak to him. But he replied to the man who told him, 'Who is my mother, and who are my brothers?' And stretching out his hand toward his disciples, he said, 'Here are my mother and my brothers! For whoever does the will of my Father in heaven is my brother, and sister, and mother' " (Matt. 12:46–50).

Witness in the Community

Witness in the community by the fellowship involves response to God's mission in the immediate community in which the fellowship lives. An individual in the community has the opportunity to witness through home, school, and job. In addition, he has the opportunity to witness by attaching himself to community structures concerned with labor, industry, politics, education, social action, etc.

Finally, witness in the community provides the opportunity for the corporate life of the fellowship to witness to mission through both its stance and its action. In this connection, the fellowship can support the cause of the poor through programs for better employment, housing, education, and social services. An extension of this support may take the form of financial and personal support of city, state, and national councils of churches or other interdenominational and secular expressions.

Witness in the World

Witness in the world by the fellowship involves both individual and group response to God's mission in the world. The world includes all seven continents, and the church must be responsive to God's work in that world beyond the need to nurture the fellowship. The individual can find one opportunity for expression of mission in the world through financial and service support of the mission enterprise of his denomination. This may be support of colleges, seminaries, hospitals, social service centers, and new congregations.

Special inner-city projects and experimental forms of congregational life, especially among minority and underprivileged peoples, provide other opportunities for expression of mission.

In addition, the individual can aid the overseas mission work of his denomination or share in ecumenical mission programs; or he can support secular work carried on by such groups as the United Nations Children's Fund (UNICEF), Japan International University, American Leprosy Mission, or various scholarship programs. Such support is well in line with the Christian's responsibility to give help to the needy.

An individual or fellowship can also support mission by providing financial resources so that an individual can serve a one- or two-year term as a doctor, nurse, builder, laborer, or teacher in one of the many nations of the world. In fact, many individuals volunteer their own talents in such service. This, too, is mission.

Summary

God is at work in the world through his church. He is at work through both individuals and the fellowship. It is important that the church discover and become involved in responding to God's mission in the whole world.

PART II

The Christian Church (Disciples of Christ)

4

Building on the Past

The Christian Church (Disciples of Christ) is a part of the "whole family of God on earth"[1] and as such continues to seek to be a partaking and participating fellowship in God's mission in the world. Historically, this church is recognized as having begun in 1809 at the Brush Run Church, Buffalo, Pennsylvania. Thomas and Alexander Campbell, father and son, are credited as its founders and early leaders. Alexander Campbell's leadership of the church for more than half a century (1809–66) is undisputed. Campbell did not speak for all the congregations, but his influence was primary in the thought and life of the church. This fact is important for any understanding of the positions of the congregations associated in the church.

This book is not designed to give a detailed history of the Christian Church (Disciples of Christ). However, this chapter was written to indicate that the leaders and congrega-

1. Preamble, *A Provisional Design for the Christian Church (Disciples of Christ)*. The *Design* was approved by the International Convention of Christian Churches (Disciples of Christ), Kansas City, Missouri, 1968. Copies may be secured from the General Office, Christian Church (Disciples of Christ), 222 S. Downey Avenue, Indianapolis, Indiana 46219.

tions of the past were involved in the struggle to respond to God's mission in the world and that congregations today can build on that past.

Founding and Early Development

The beginning of the Christian Church (Disciples of Christ) in 1809 came about for three important reasons. First, Thomas and Alexander Campbell were deeply disturbed by the divisions that separated the church of their native Scotland. They viewed these divisions as scandalous and committed themselves to finding and developing the means of healing the brokenness of the church. Second, a practical problem had arisen in the area of the western frontier of the early nineteenth century. Ministers were scarce and congregations languished for lack of their services of baptism, communion, and preaching. Third, the Campbells had gained insight from their scholarly studies of the Scriptures that led them to the position that congregations, as a part of the body of Christ, had all the authority needed to elect their own leaders. Consequently, the rapidly developing frontier was provided with the necessary leaders—normally called "elders"—for establishing and developing congregations.

Alexander Campbell's position is evidenced in these words:

> ... the government of the church is an absolute monarchy, and the Lord Jesus Christ is the absolute monarch, on whose shoulders is the government and in whose hands are the reins.... his will, published in the New Testament, is the sole law of the church; and ... every society or assembly, meeting once every week in one place, according to this law, or the commandments of this king, requires no other head....[2]

2. Alexander Campbell, ed., *The Christian Baptist,* 15th ed., rev. by D. S. Burnet from the 2d ed., with Campbell's last corrections, 7 vols. in 1 (St. Louis: Christian Publishing Co., n.d.), 1:25 (entry for Nov. 3, 1823).

It is clear that Campbell had found a way to establish congregations, especially in the frontier setting. It remained for such men as "Raccoon" John Smith, Walter Scott, and Barton W. Stone to capture the Western Reserve (Ohio), Kentucky, Illinois, and Indiana and to release the force of the new message out across the plains to the shores of the Pacific.

One of the consequences of Campbell's position was the development of strong congregational autonomy. Each congregation was complete within itself. Association with other congregations was on a voluntary basis. Personal salvation and individual congregational concern were the hallmarks of the Christian Church from 1809 to 1849.

Before 1849 there were second thoughts about the strong development of congregational autonomy. Sixteen years after Campbell wrote in *The Christian Baptist* concerning congregational autonomy, he wrote these words in *The Christian System*:

> Still, all these particular congregations of the Lord, ... though equally independent of one another as to the management of their own peculiar affairs, are, by virture of one common Lord, one faith, one baptism, and one common salvation, but one kingdom or church of God, and, as such, are under obligations to co-operate with one another in all measures promotive of the great ends of Christ's death and resurrection.[3]

Expansion and Growth

In 1849 the American Christian Missionary Society was organized in Cincinnati, Ohio. It was the first of several organizations of the Christian Church (Disciples of Christ) that made it possible for the congregations to work together to support one another and establish new churches and en-

3. *The Christian System,* 2d ed. (Cincinnati: Central Book Concern, 1839), p. 73.

gage in Christian education, higher education, and social concerns—to mention only a few of the mission enterprises. By 1874 the Christian Woman's Board of Missions was founded, and in 1875 the Foreign Christian Missionary Society was created.

Each of these organizations and the concerns that each represented were designed to provide the congregations with increased means of working together. By so working together, they could respond to God's mission in the nineteenth-century world. Thus, the struggle to overcome congregational autonomy was begun and would continue to the present day, although with somewhat diminished intensity. The freedom of the congregation in cooperative work with others was forging ahead.

Becoming a Church

Controversy between the supporters of congregational autonomy and those supporting congregational cooperation was strong in the period 1920–68. The congregations and their mission boards and societies, however, sought increased means of working together in response to God's mission and in 1919 organized the United Christian Missionary Society. The United Society was an organization with three important purposes. First, it brought together the majority of the organized agencies of the Christian Church (Disciples of Christ) for the first time in their history; second, the establishment of new congregations was supported through the United Society; and third, the regional (state/area) organizations were undergirded. The very breadth and inclusiveness of the United Society gave birth to a new concept of church within the Christian Churches which gave a new dynamic to becoming church.

Congregations were coming to understand their new sense

of power as they worked together to respond to God's mission. However, they lacked, among other things, a common style of internal organization that would improve their individual participation in mission. It was Willard M. Wickizer, Sr., for more than a quarter of a century one of the foremost leaders of the Disciples of Christ, who brought the form of that organization into being through what was known in the 1940s (and still is) as "functional" church organization.[4]

The purpose of this style of organization was to provide the congregation with ways to bring to bear its maximum power in response to God's mission through all phases of its work—Christian education, worship, evangelism, social welfare, membership development, world outreach, stewardship, use and care of property—and through auxiliary organizations of men, women, and youth. This plan of organization made possible the emancipation of congregations from the self-interest of their own autonomy. It also provided the opportunity for more effective and cooperative work in the world.

For the Disciples of Christ the decade of the 1960s was described as the "Decade of Decision," and that it was. It was a time of searching, struggling, and reaching for new forms of life that would enable the congregation more fully to engage in God's mission and would bring the church together in all its manifestations—congregational, regional (state/area), and general (national and international). In this context it was natural that one of the major achievements of the 1960s was the approval by the International Convention meeting in Kansas City, Missouri, of the Provisional Design for the Christian Church (Disciples of Christ). The Provisional Design is the latest development in the strug-

4. *See* Willard M. Wickizer, *A Functional Church Organization,* rev. ed. (Indianapolis: Department of Church Development and Evangelism of the United Christian Missionary Society; St. Louis: Christian Board of Publication, 1957).

gle of the Christian Church to become a reality and of the congregation to fulfill its potential. This achievement is not a conclusion but a beginning, and the end is not in view. It does, however, encourage a renewal of the congregation and other manifestations of the church in response to God's mission in the world.

Timeless Issues

Individuals and congregations of the Christian Church (Disciples of Christ), whether or not they realize it, are the product of its history. They are inheritors of a movement that sought and still seeks to be relevant to the great issues of man's life. Obviously, not all issues of yesterday are critical for today. Many, however, seem to be relevant to every age. The church, from its beginning, has faced the issues of man's rebellion against God and man, and man's innate sinfulness, especially in the areas of Christian unity, the right of conscience, justice, political order, human dignity, and peace.

Christian Unity

The concern for and commitment to the cause of Christian unity took two directions in the Christian Church (Disciples of Christ): first, the unity of congregations working together; and, second, the unity of the whole family of God on earth.

The unity of congregations working together cooperatively, as we have seen, was a struggle to overcome congregational autonomy with ordered working together in response to God's mission.

Unity of the church as the "whole family of God on earth" was the foundation of Thomas Campbell's *Declaration and Address* (1809), in which he declared that the church is "essentially, intentionally and constitutionally one." Later, Alexander Campbell was to expand this position. Winfred E. Garrison, in *Religion Follows the Frontier,* points out, "... there was a decided revival of interest in Christian union among the Disciples about 1900, and in this respect they did not stand alone."[5] Among those who led in this interest were F. D. Power, J. B. Briney, J. H. Garrison, and Peter Ainslie. In 1910 a Council of Christian Union was authorized and organized.

Foreign missionaries began to work together across denominational lines and were quickly joined in ecumenical work by the American mission and religious education forces. The Christian Church (Disciples of Christ) became a part of the Federal Council of Churches, one of the twelve organizations that united to become the National Council of the Churches of Christ in the U.S.A. The Christian Church became a part of the International Missionary Council and the World Sunday School Association. The last two organizations were to become part of the World Council of Churches, of which the Christian Church was a founding member. Currently, the Christian Church is participating in the Consultation on Church Union (COCU), begun in 1960. There has been and continues to be strong support of the conciliar movement at city and state levels.

Conscience

The right of conscience is presently much in the thought and action of the world, especially as it relates to such matters as military service, law and order, abortion, and choice of political expression. Conscience was important to Alexander Campbell, as indicated by these words: " ... from what source derive we a conviction of our duty? Is it from conscience? By no means.... Conscience, according to Paul, ac-

5. (New York: Harper & Brothers, 1931), p. 280.

cuses and excuses. But by what standard? That is the question."[6] From another Campbell writing, we read: *"The law of love is the supreme law of religion, morality, and expediency. No code of laws, without it, could make or keep any people ... peaceable, and happy....* We cannot love by law, but we can walk in love with no other law but that of love."[7]

Justice

Justice in the affairs of men was given considerable attention by Alexander Campbell. He was a landowner and operated a large farm. He was concerned with the roots of economic life which rest in justice and the affairs of human dealing. He wrote, "Justice, it is agreed on all hands, is a fundamental virtue, and the basis of all social qualities that adorn and bless human nature."[8] Again, he wrote:

> If, then, a lie may be told, and injustice done in word, but not in deed—in form, but not in substance—then is the defaulter innocent in one point, but guilty in another—innocent in doing all that was expected at the time, but guilty of using language which according to its fair construction, and according to its acceptation and obligation in innumerable instances, means the very opposite of what he intends.[9]

Political Order

Political order was important to Campbell. He served in the Virginia legislature and the Virginia Constitutional Convention. He was a follower of John Locke; and in 1851 he wrote as follows: "In the affairs of this life—in all temporal and earthly matters—the civil law, the social compact, is our

6. *Millennial Harbinger,* 1862, p. 110.
7. *The Christian System,* p. 94.
8. *Millennial Harbinger,* 1838, p. 386.
9. Ibid., p. 389.

rule of action. In religion, in faith, in piety, God alone is Lord of the conscience."[10]

The very soul of politics is cold calculating selfishness. The policy ... which the statesman hails with any sort of enthusiasm, is the protective system.... An individual who would apply to his domestic interests in reference to his neighbors, the same arguments which call for loud huzzas in the senate chamber ... would damn himself at home in the estimation of his neighbors. ... The unsocial maxim of the English statesman, which has been well studied in this country, is, "Wring from the hand that guides a *foreign* loom the last farthing, provided only it enhance the value of a *domestic* shuttle." ... 'Tis thus that nations become great, and it is thus that the individuals which compose nations "worry and devour each other."[11]

Human Dignity

Slavery of the Negro was a relevant issue in the time and life of Alexander Campbell. It is important to note that in spite of financial loss Campbell set free from slavery "every human being that came in any way under my influence or was my property."[12]

In 1845 Campbell took a strong position against slavery and in favor of a "gradual termination" of the practice, which he described as abusive and an impoverishment upon the states and communities.

In connection with the matter of human dignity it is worth including the following statement:

As an American citizen, I have my opinions upon the policy and honor of the institution [slavery]; but these can neither sanction, nor annul, nor modify my Christian obligations. I neither assume to be an apologist for American slavery, a reformer, nor an abolitionist of American slavery. The laws sustain

10. Ibid, 1851, p. 30.
11. Ibid., 1832, p. 115.
12. Ibid., 1845, p. 259.

it; and so long as the laws sustain it, abstractly right or wrong, it is the duty of every *Christian* man to respect it and to offer it no violence whatever. A Christian may, indeed, seek by his vote to have it annihilated or modified; but he cannot, as a law-abiding citizen or a Christian, violate or tempt others to violate existing laws without offending his Lord and becoming obnoxious to his displeasure.[13]

Peace

Condemnation of war and support of peace were strong in the life of Alexander Campbell. In 1848 he wrote: "War is not now, nor was it ever, a process of justice. It never was a test of truth—a criterion of right."[14]

Concern for peace led to this constructive suggestion from Campbell:

Could not a united National Court be made as feasible and as practicable as a United States Court? Why not, as often proposed, and as eloquently, ably, and humanely argued by the advocates of peace, have a Congress of Nations and a High Court of Nations for adjudicating and terminating all international misunderstandings and complaints, redressing and remedying all wrongs and grievances?[15]

Campbell, a leader of his time, and his words regarding an organization of the nations of the world, are only now beginning to be heard and understood.

The quotations about these issues of the nineteeth century are all too brief, but they do provide a glimpse of a leader of the Christian church seeking to set the direction and create a style of life that responded to God's mission and came face to face with the vital issues in his world and time. The Chris-

13. Ibid., pp. 108–9.
14. Ibid., 1848, p. 377.
15. Ibid., pp. 382–83.

tian church in the twentieth century must be as relevant to its world as was the life and work of Alexander Campbell to the nineteenth century.

Summary

The Christian Church (Disciples of Christ) has struggled for a clearer meaning and improved work of the congregation as a part of the church. Its history reflects that struggle, and the congregations today are a part of that history. In addition, the church and its leaders sought more than a century ago to be relevant to the issues of the world. The church today is the product of its heritage and is called as the recipient of its history to respond to God's mission in today's world.

5

Characteristics of the Congregation as Church

Congregations are found in open country, villages, towns, and cities. The majority of them can be classified as "traditional" and as being an assembly (or group) of persons affiliated with a denomination or other religious body, gathered together for religious worship, instruction, and service. They may hold property, have a set meeting place, and perform acts of service directed to the nurture of the group and the world.

In light of the thrust of church renewal since 1945 and the developing reform or revolution in the church and the congregations, new meanings of *congregation* are evident. One definition could be as follows: a group of people who assemble to discover what God is doing in the world and to respond to this "calling" of God through a life of servanthood in the world. The characteristics of this type of congregation have been identified by Rüdiger Reitz as (1) "experimentation as the life style of the church"; (2) belief in "the inadequacy of traditional modes of thought and existing structures"; (3) belief that "contemporary church renewal gets its driving power from the conviction that the church ought to display ethical responsibility for society."[1]

1. *The Church in Experiment* (New York: Abingdon Press, 1969), p. 16.

The understanding of congregation as being the assembly of God's people is very old. The congregation is called the synagogue in the Old Testament. The traditional congregation today, like the synagogue of old, is a group of people celebrating in worship the mighty acts of God, living in fellowship (koinonia), and teaching and learning the meanings of God revealed in Jesus Christ and the world.

According to the King James translation, the word *congregation* appears only once in the New Testament, in Acts 13:43: "Now when the congregation was broken up, many of the Jews and religious proselytes followed Paul and Barnabas: who, speaking to them, persuaded them to continue in the grace of God." The Revised Standard Version does not use the word *congregation*. Although there are no other references to congregation in the King James Version of the New Testament, there are many references to church *(ekklesia)*. In this sense, the church is the people of God as they respond to his calling and become the "called out," partaking and participating in God's mission (see chapter 3).

Emil Brunner writes:

> In speaking of the one body, Paul speaks of the "Church" without using the word. For what Paul denotes by the word ecclesia, which is normally translated as Church, is just this: the fellowship of believers, the people of the Christ in their unity. Their unity is Christ, their diversity the different kinds of believers with their gifts and services. The unity of the Community demands exactly the recognition of this difference and the observance of the frontiers that result from it. Each one is to do what God has allotted to him through his specific talent as a particular task.[2]

2. From *The Letter to the Romans,* by Emil Brunner, translated by H. A. Kennedy, p. 104. Published in the U.S.A. by The Westminster Press, 1959. © 1959, Lutterworth Press. Used by permission.

The life and work of today's congregation is more complex than that of either the synagogue of the Old Testament or the church of the New Testament. This is so for one reason: the synagogue of the Old Testament operated under the umbrella of the Temple in Jerusalem. The congregation today is the church at work in the community. The New Testament church is more like what today's congregation is struggling to become. The church in the first century sought to gather together those who responded to the will of God and send them out into the world. Today's congregation is responsible for both the Christian life of individuals within its fellowship and the expression of its Christian influence in the life of the community and the world.

An understanding of what today's congregation is may be gained from consideration of what it is not.

First, the congregation is not an end in itself. Unfortunately, many congregations are content with worship and study and leave service to the world for others to accomplish. Such "turned-inness" gives them the appearance of private clubs designed for the special privilege of their members. In this connection the affluent have, at times, used the congregation to defend their special interests, while the poor have used it as an escape from reality. For both, the congregation has lost its "called-outness" and has become subjected to the will of man.

Second, the congregation is not a building. The early Christians gathered in homes. A nineteenth-century congregation in the United States typically began as a group of people meeting in a home and soon moving to a schoolhouse or some other public building. The first church buildings were modest, some even austere, in their structure and appearance. Each congregation in its own way sought to magnify the celebration of the mighty acts of God in worship and study. Following World War II, the building of new churches increased rapidly. Affluence, larger population, and population mobility were some of the contributing factors. In this same era the number of dollars spent on cushioned pews, pipe organs, and other evidences of opulence increased rapidly. Often, the congregation became identified more with a building than with its mission.

Third, the congregation is not just an organization. This is not to say that organization is unnecessary—quite the contrary. Whenever one individual joins with another and they with others to do the will of God, it is necessary for them to have the means to carry out in an orderly and proper manner what they understand to be God's will. This requires organization. Problems arise when organization becomes more important than the mission to be accomplished. Organization should be designed to enable the congregation to achieve its response to God's mission. It should be dictated by the needs of the situation, but it should also be flexible and capable of change. Jesus had something to say which might be applied to the congregation that has become a slave to any particular form of organizational life, when he declared, "The sabbath was made for man, not man for the sabbath" (Mark 2:27).

If these are a few of the things that the congregation is not, then what exactly is the congregation—what are its vital characteristics? Characteristics of the congregation as church may be understood as being of two kinds, both of which are basically theological. The first kind has to do with theology and the second with applied theology. These two kinds of characteristics are two sides of the same coin. To deal with theology apart from its application is to reduce the Christian life to contemplation and thought. To deal with applied theology apart from theology is to see the Christian life only as method, structure, and action. Theology is the source from which flows applied theological action.

Theological Characteristics

Theological characteristics of the congregation as church may be understood in terms of *love, mission,* and *servanthood.* These three central characteristics require the church to accept the lordship of God revealed in Jesus Christ and to respond faithfully to God's mission.

Love

Love as expressed in the New Testament is a characteristic central to all others. The centrality of love is evident in the following passages of scripture:

> "For God so loved the world that he gave his only Son, that whoever believes in him should not perish but have eternal life" (John 3:16).
>
> "But love your enemies, and do good, and lend, expecting nothing in return; and your reward will be great, and you will be sons of the Most High; for he is kind to the ungrateful and the selfish" (Luke 6:35).
>
> "A new commandment I give to you, that you love one another; even as I have loved you, that you also love one another" (John 13:34).
>
> "This is my commandment, that you love one another as I have loved you. Greater love has no man than this, that a man lay down his life for his friends" (John 15:12–13).

The kind of love mentioned in each of these quotations is selfless and outgoing. It seeks not its own satisfaction. It is directed toward the good of others. It is the kind of love that gave man the revelation of God in the life of Jesus Christ. It is the kind of love that made it possible for Christ to respond to a cross as a symbol of the Father's love and man's need.

Love, as a characteristic of the congregation as church, expresses itself in a variety of ways. Some of these are: the response of the individual to the will of God, the development and support of each member of the fellowship in Christlike growth, the response of the congregation to the will of God, and the opening of opportunities for mutual development of the Christian life with those beyond the congregation in the whole world. As a primary and central characteristic of the congregation, love makes such exciting experiences both possible and necessary.

Mission

Mission is a second theological characteristic of the congregation as church. Mission is making evident the love of God by the individual and the congregation. It is the response of the individual and congregation to God's mission.

Mission is the "sentness" (see chapter 3) of the congregation expressed through the individual members and the corporate body. In the Acts of the Apostles, Paul describes "sentness" in the Damascus Road experience. From the moment he encountered Christ, the persecutor of the Christians became their advocate. Paul was under new orders from a new Master. He became a missionary partaking of and participating in God's mission.

The high dedication and consecration required of individuals and congregations accepting their "sentness" may be seen in the life of Telemachus as he sought to increase awareness of the value of human life and to reconcile man to God. Increasingly convinced that sacrificing human beings to wild animals was wrong, especially in the gladiatorial games of ancient Rome, he determined to express both his Christian faith and his opposition to acts of destruction.

In the year 404 a gladiatorial program celebrated at Rome the dubious victory of Stilicho at Pollentia. Blood had begun to flow when an Oriental monk, Telemachus, leaped from the stands into the arena and demanded that the combats cease. The infuriated spectators stoned him to death; but the Emperor Honorius, moved by the scene, issued an edict abolishing gladiatorial games.[3]

Individuals and the congregation have been involved in the "sentness" of mission among the poor, the affluent, the laborer, the warrior, the merchant, and God's other children near and far.

The congregation as church must accept its mission. It should not deceive itself at this point. The congregation is not to accept the mission of its own choosing, but the mission of God as the congregation *understands* what God wants it to do and to be.

Servanthood

Servanthood is a third theological characteristic of the congregation. This characteristic is mentioned in the New Testament in several forms, three of which are as follows:

> "and whoever would be first among you must be your slave; even as the Son of man came not to be served but to serve, and to give his life as a ransom for many" (Matt. 20:27-28).
>
> "Well done, good and faithful servant; you have been faithful over a little, I will set you over much ... " (Matt. 25:23).
>
> (The Greek word for servant or slave in the above two passages is *doulos*. This word means one who is bound by another or pressed into service by another.)

3. Will Durant, *The Age of Faith,* Story of Civilization, vol. 4 (New York: Simon & Schuster, 1950), p. 31.

"You yourselves know how I lived among you all the time from the first day that I set foot in Asia, serving the Lord with all humility and with tears ..." (Acts 20:18–19).

The point is clear from these words of both Christ and Paul that the role of the servant is one which God has set as appropriate for man in his response to God's mission. The role of the servant is one which the congregation is to accept. Otherwise it is not fulfilling the distinctive characteristic of servanthood to God and man.

The servant is concerned about the good of his master and seeks to do his master's will. The congregation as servant seeks to respond to God's will—to do his will.

Applied Theological Characteristics

The theological characteristics of the congregation as church can become effective only when their meaning is made evident in the day-to-day life of the individual members and in the congregation itself. Thus, certain applied theological characteristics of the congregation as church may be understood as theology in action and may be put in two categories: *nurture* and *action*. Nurture and action are not separate areas of concern. On the contrary, nurture blends into action and action frequently motivates nurture. In addition, both may be understood as Christian witness. This fact must be kept clearly in mind in dealing with these concerns in the congregation.

Nurture, as a concern of the congregation, has both congregational and extracongregational implications. On the one hand, the fellowship (koinonia) has to be nurtured in the faith; and, on the other hand, the very experiences that nurture the life of the fellowship form much of the thrust of the congregation in witness beyond its own life into the whole world.

Keeping in mind the interrelatedness of nurture and action and the congregational and extracongregational implications of both, let us consider the program elements that make possible the working of the will of God in the life of the individual and the corporate life of the congregation as church. These elements, arbitrarily separated under nurture and action, are:

Nurture	*Action*
Evangelism and Churchmanship	Social Involvement
Education	Stewardship
Worship	Outreach

Nurture

Nurture, as used in this book, refers to that which nourishes and provides for growth of the individual and corporate life of the congregation in learning and training experiences of renewed spiritual living. Nurture may include the meditative, academic, and action experiences of the individual and congregation in daily life. It is directed toward the spiritual renewal of the internal life of the individual and the corporate fellowship, and toward the extracongregational life and witness of the congregation.

Applying this definition of nurture to the three program elements listed above can lead to a clearer understanding of the congregation as church in responding to God's mission. At this point, however, the application will be brief, with a more detailed treatment provided in Part III, chapters 9 through 14.

Evangelism. Evangelism is the proclamation of the Good News of God, inviting all individuals and the corporate life of the congregation to respond to his mission. Theologically, it involves pronouncement of the gospel, repentance, confession, and dedication to Christian service in the world. In application, evangelism is responsible for confronting every individual with the "calling out" of God and, thereby, securing the enlistment of all who respond to God's "calling" in support of his mission. Evangelism is essential to the strength and ongoing life of Christian service in the whole world.

Education. Education is the involvement in that learning process which makes possible the discovery of new meanings in life. Such new meanings are viable when they emerge out of man's persistent life needs as they are confronted and penetrated by the revelation of God in the life of Jesus Christ.

Education is the equipping of the laity for response to God's mission. Equipping the laity for mission is built upon the commitment of the individual and may serve as one means for the proclamation of the Good News.

Learning experiences may take place in and outside the congregation. Curriculum materials and leadership training may serve as two methods of equipping the laity.

Education is more than abstract or academic learning. Education must be academically sound in content and techniques; but more importantly, it must be designed to direct the individual and the congregation toward the carrying out of the will of God in the world and the maintenance of both the individual and corporate life of the congregation in that mission.

Worship. Worship is the celebration of the mighty acts of God in history. The use of the word *history* at this point includes not only the past, but also the present and the future. Worship, therefore, celebrates what God has done in the past, is doing in the world today, and may do in the future. If the individual and the congregation celebrate only what God has done in the past, then worship is directed to a God who is in the past and is now dead. If the individual and the congregation celebrate only what God is doing today, then worship is directed to a God without meaning from the past or a design for the future. If the individual and congregation celebrate only what may be revealed in the future, then worship lacks concrete reality for the present.

Worship is a personal experience of God revealed in Jesus Christ, the mystery and greatness of the God of history. Worship should have historical perspective which includes the past, present, and future. This means that it should always be open to individual expressions—or group expressions—of new forms of worship. Opposition to new forms would indicate a belief that God reveals himself only in certain unchanging forms which, if followed by rote, assure the worshiper of a kind of magic formula for knowing—possibly controlling—God.

Worship must be concerned with both individual growth and the nurture of the congregation. Consequently, worship moves from the personal experience of meditation and study to corporate experiences of formal and informal worship; and each may reinforce the other.

Essentially, worship, especially worship services, provides the opportunity for the individual and the congregation to grow in the fellowship (koinonia) and witness to the world through their response to and development in God's mission.

Action

Action is the second area of applied theological characteristics of the congregation as church. This does not mean that action is not a part of the area denoted as nurture. As a matter of fact, evangelism, education, and worship are directed to action, and, if they do not result in action, they are incomplete.

Social involvement. Through social involvement, the individual and the congregation find meaningful expression.

The Good News of God must have practical expression through the individual life and through the life and work of the congregation. Such practical expression is evidenced in these words:

> " ... preach good news to the poor.
> ... proclaim release to the captives
> and recovering of sight to the blind,
> ... set at liberty those who are oppressed,
> ... proclaim the acceptable year of the Lord."
>
> —Luke 4:18–19

The congregation that joins its resources of persons (power) and wealth (power) provides answers to human need at home and in the world. It can change structures and systems of society. This is the kind of action that calls forth new commitments and new understanding of what the congregation is as the "called out" people of God.

Stewardship. Stewardship, from the standpoint of the congregation, is essentially commitment of the church member to God and total participation in support of the mission of the church. It requires deliberate and responsible sharing of abilities and money. Stewardship is premised upon the fact that God has given man life and the necessities to sustain that life. It remains for man to express his thanksgiving for these gifts. How man uses his life and how he uses his treasure are ruled by his commitment to God and expressed in a life of thanksgiving. Out of his total commitment of life and treasure, the individual sets aside a portion—ideally a minimum of 10 percent—for the carrying out of God's will through the congregation to the world.

There is, in addition to the responsibility of personal stewardship, the responsibility of congregational stewardship. The congregation is responsible for the use of its life and substance, God's gift to the fellowship. The most obvious expression of responsible stewardship for the congregation is its involvement in redemptive community service and in sharing its treasure for the purpose of service in the world. The congregation that takes seriously its responsibility as steward may have to choose between padded pews and providing better housing in the ghetto, between a new building with a new pipe organ and staffing a hospital in Africa, or between carpeting the sanctuary and supporting a school in Indonesia. In yet a different way, the congregation may have to choose between protecting its own life and risking that life by social and political involvement in issues in the community where the congregation is situated.

In every instance, the point of decision for the individual and the congregation rests upon whether there is involvement first in God's mission or in choosing to do what seems desirable from a human point of view.

Outreach. Outreach helps the individual and the congregation to identify with the mission of God as expressed by Jesus, the proclamation of the Good News to the poor and the affluent. This Good News offers tangible and concrete hope to God's hungry people as it speaks to their need of livelihood. It proclaims release from the captivity of tradition and superstition and offers new freedoms in a Christian understanding of the universe. It shares a redemptive hope as it demonstrates God's love and concern for men and introduces them to a saving and transforming faith.

The individual and congregation involved in outreach discover an exciting and meaningful response to God's mission. The individual can no longer take refuge behind the flimsy excuse of concern for those "at home." The poor are at home and they are also all around the world. The poor must be served, and the evil of poverty must be broken by overseas mission abroad, and through social involvement at home.

Ignorance at home is ignorance in the world, and the slavery of ignorance must be expunged in the light of learning. Prejudice at home is prejudice in the world, and the evil of prejudice cannot be erased by those who serve the members of another race halfway around the world and ignore those in the ghetto in their own city. Did not Jesus once say: "You are the light of the world. A city set on a hill cannot be hid. Nor do men light a lamp and put it under a bushel, but on a stand, and it gives light to all in the house. Let your light so shine before men, that they may see your good works and give glory to your Father who is in heaven" (Matt. 5:14–16).

Summary

The congregation as church is the people of God called to his mission and responding to all people in the world. The characteristics of love, mission, servanthood, nurture, and action make the congregation different from all other social groups. The difference is not in organization, but in acceptance of God's mission so that the light of God may shine in the world for the healing of men and nations.

6

Tools for the Congregation

The congregation's response to God's mission in the world requires understanding of the personnel and instrumentalities available for engaging in and implementing mission. These are the tools the congregation utilizes in its work.

Personnel

Personnel is of two kinds: leaders and the members of the congregation working together in mission. Leadership is considered in this chapter. The congregation will be dealt with in chapter 8, "The Minister and Laity in Mission."

Leadership

Leadership is the key to the congregation's effective response to God's mission. Congregations are responsible for identifying, selecting, training, and maintaining its leaders.

Congregational leadership is aided by the general (national and international) offices of the church as they develop creative techniques and materials to identify, select, and train leaders. The general manifestation[1] of the church also provides guidance in planning program and preparing supporting materials.

Regional (state/area) offices provide similar help to leaders. They interpret and sometimes modify resources to meet the needs peculiar to the region and its congregations. Regional offices also provide an important channel of communication between the congregation and the general manifestations of the church designed to strengthen the congregation's response to God's mission.

Identifying leadership needs. Identifying the leadership needs of the congregation requires a careful study of the total tasks being undertaken, and needing to be undertaken, by the congregation in fulfillment of its mission. Begin with an inventory such as the one on the following page.

1. *Manifestation* is a word used to describe the general (national and international), regional (state/area), and congregational expressions of the Christian Church (Disciples of Christ). For a study of these three manifestations, see *A Provisional Design for the Christian Church (Disciples of Christ).*

CURRENT CONGREGATIONAL LEADERSHIP

Principal Staff

- Minister(s)
- Organist(s)
- Choir leader(s)
- Custodian(s)
- Secretary(ies)
- Other

Group Leaders

- Elders, including chairman
- Deacons and deaconesses, including chairmen
- General Board, including chairman
- Congregational Steering Committee or Cabinet, including chairman
- Committee (department) chairmen and members
- Teachers and leaders in the congregation's educational ministry
- Officers and group leaders in auxiliary groups of the congregation, such as Christian Women's Fellowship, Christian Men's Fellowship, youth group(s), etc.
- Task group chairmen and members (Committees fulfill the congregation's response to God's mission in terms of the characteristics of the congregation as church—evangelism, education, stewardship, worship, outreach, property, membership development, etc.)

(All leadership should be specifically identified, and adequate representation of youth and women should be provided in all areas of work.)

Filling leadership needs in the congregation will be less difficult if the congregation takes a survey of its leadership potential and maintains an up-to-date working file concerning it. A card such as the following would be helpful in preparing such a survey:

LEADERSHIP POTENTIAL SURVEY CARD

Name____________________________________

Address__________________________________

Telephone__________________Age_____Sex________

Leadership Experiences________________________

____

____

Leadership Training:

Training Needed___________________________

____

In-service Training________________________

____

Courses Taken____________________________

____

Academic Training:

_____High School

_____College

_____Other

Type of Service Preferred_____________________

____

The reverse side of the Leadership Potential Survey Card may be used to record the leadership training of, and leadership accepted by, the individual.

When the leadership needs have been identified, job descriptions developed, and the survey of leadership potential completed, the congregation is ready for the next step: to place its leadership needs beside its leadership potential and determine where and what kind of programs are needed by the congregation in order to upgrade and develop its leaders to the fullest possible extent.

The following chart may be helpful in this final step of identifying leadership needs:[2]

OUR LEADERSHIP NEEDS 197—					
1. Program		2. Organization		3. Responsibilities Beyond Our Congregation	
Project/ Activity Served	Leaders Needed	Group Served	Leaders Needed	Group/ Activity Served	Leaders Needed

The above chart will provide an overall picture of the

2. Adapted from Richard E. Lentz, *Solving Leadership Problems* (St. Louis: Christian Board of Publication, n.d.), p. 15.

congregation's response to God's mission and related leadership needs. Column 1 provides the opportunity to list the congregation's specific program and required leadership. Column 2 is for the listing of various organizations of the congregation and identifying required leadership. Column 3 provides the opportunity to list responsibilities outside the congregation in such areas as local community service; district, regional (state/area), general (national and international) service; and ecumenical concerns, and the required leadership.

With leadership needs of the congregation identified, attention should be turned to the development of appropriate leadership training programs. These may be developed and conducted denominationally, interdenominationally, in cooperation with regional leadership programs, or by some combination of these. A study of *Foundations for Teaching Church Leaders* will make possible the training of leaders in terms of general needs for all leaders and skill needs for leaders of special responsibilities of the congregation.[3]

Instrumentalities

Instrumentalities for engaging in and implementing mission may be described under the headings of procedural tools and physical tools. Procedural tools are planning, research, coordination, and evaluation. Physical tools are program materials, buildings, and equipment.

Procedural Tools

Planning. Planning is the development of the congregation's blueprint for action in response to God's mission. Planning will be strengthened if the congregation understands what its planning function is in relation to the general (na-

3. *Foundations for Teaching Church Leaders* is the title of the leader development materials for the Christian Life Curriculum, Christian Board of Publication, St. Louis, Missouri.

tional and international) and regional (state/area) manifestations of the Christian Church (Disciples of Christ). At the outset it needs to be understood that the general and regional manifestations of the church share with the congregation the common purpose and goals of the Christian Church (Disciples of Christ). They mutually support each other, and seek to strengthen the vital unity and extend the mission of the church and the congregation.

Persons responsible for national program-planning offer suggested program and supporting resources to regions and to congregations. Regions engage in planning designed to develop programs necessary for the mission of the church in specific regions, making appropriate use of those programs and resources developed at the general level (see Appendix B for suggestions concerning planning functions of the national, regional, and congregational manifestations of the church).

Planning takes into account the resources of available time, personnel (clergy and laity), space, and funds. Planning has long been recognized by government and industry as imperative to meaningful action, but it is relatively new in congregations.

The development and maintenance of a congregational calendar that lists all events in the life of the congregation is essential in planning. The calendar should be kept in a central place. Only authorized persons should be permitted to add or delete a date once the congregation's program and calendar are approved.

Program-planning for the congregation will be most effective when it encompasses an extended period of time. It should project careful planning for a minimum of a biennial time span, and envision broad objectives for at least an additional biennial time span. The current biennium for which planning is needed should have specific, detailed plans for program, projects, and events. The additional biennium should be planned in broad outline form.

Resources for congregational planning are available from regional and general manifestations of the church (see Appendix A):

- Church program guidance developed by the general manifestation of the church[4]
- Information concerning specific programs and procedures developed by the general manifestation of the church and communicated in original or modified form by the regional manifestation of the church[5]
- Information concerning specific programs and procedures developed by the regional manifestation of the church[6]

Additional resources are:

- Information developed by the congregation as a result of evaluation and research regarding its own programs
- Information derived from other congregations of the same denomination or other denominations
- Information from ecumenical sources[7]

Program-planning should cover the total life of the congregation and set forth specific program goals that are *measurable and reasonably achievable.* Projects, programs, and events of all committees and groups should be set forth with dates, hours, places, leaders, and equipment identified. All personnel should be committed prior to placing their names in the final report of the planning group. In following this procedure the entire congregational program is given, including

4. See *Church Program Guidance Manuals* and *Annual Planning Guide and Calendar* (Indianapolis: National Church Program Coordinating Council). See also *Vanguard,* the quarterly program journal for congregational leaders.

5. See *Vanguard.*

6. *See* regional (state/area) monthly or quarterly mailings.

7. *See* city, state, National or World Council of Churches publications.

the work of constituency groups such as the Christian Women's Fellowship, Christian Men's Fellowship, youth groups, and organized church school classes or groups.

Program-planning should deal with budget needs—known and projected—to make the program operable. Without such consideration of budget needs related to program, the congregation may plan many things with little result. Such knowledge frees the congregation from building program upon program, project upon project, and event upon event, thereby limiting effective achievement. *Program should dictate budget.* All too frequently, this process is reversed—budget dictates program. The program and related budget needs should be developed simultaneously and reported to the budget committee of the congregation and to the cabinet or steering committee for coordination.

When the coordinated program and related budget needs have been prepared by the appropriate departments and committees, they are ready for presentation to the general board of the congregation for action and then to the congregation for action. When the congregation approves the program and budget, it knows quite clearly what its money will be spent for.

Planning program, projects, and events in the above manner provides possible benefits, such as:

- The involvement of many people in planning—through commissions, departments, committees, or task groups —provides a broad base for the discovery of the congregation's response and planning for response to God's mission; hence the congregation will be less likely to fall victim to a small power structure within the congregation.
- The relating of program and budget provides opportunity for developing new programs, altering operating

program, and deleting program no longer needed, in a realistic and effective way.

- This style of program-planning provides the opportunity for the congregation to respond to God's mission as a congregation and not be wholly dependent upon changing (professional) ministerial leadership. This is important since the average length of ministry is approximately three to four years.
- This style of program-planning will establish the laity as essential to the response of the congregation to God's mission. The role of the laity will be dealt with later; however, it is important to note here that this role must become more effective if the congregation's response is to be a vital force in all areas of life.

Research. Research is of two kinds: primary and secondary. Primary research is that accomplished by research centers or government agencies or provided by pooled resources of industry, voluntary and religious groups. Primary research is generally not the field of congregational endeavor. The congregation is most often the consumer of primary research. The results of this kind of research may be secured from governmental, ecumenical, or denominational research offices and research centers (see Appendix A). Primary research covers the areas of human inquiry included in secondary research, but it is generally of a scope and technical quality not achieved by secondary research.

Secondary research is the type most commonly used by congregations and is designed to provide basic data regarding the sociological, demographic, and financial background of the congregation and program participation by the members of the congregation. The techniques of survey, statistical study, and data gathering are most frequently used, even though these may be used in primary research also.

The congregation that uses either primary or secondary research needs to prepare for each research project by answering the following questions:

- *What is the purpose of the desired research?*

  The purpose should be set forth as a hypothesis to be tested, for example, a hypothesis resulting from the question, How best can theological dialogue take place between the minister and the members of the congregation?

  Such a proposition requires a research project which, among other things, discovers the theological education level of the members of the congregation, the theological issues of interest to them, and their desires regarding the theological dialogue.

- *What is the desired information?*

  Would such theological dialogue be beneficial to the life of the congregation? If so, identify the possible benefits. Identify various approaches to the development of such dialogue.

- *What is the use to be made of the desired information?*

  State in easily understood language how the information is to be used. According to the purpose in the example above, the data would be used to determine a type of program that would involve the minister and congregation in some form of theological dialogue. This might be a study and discussion centered around the minister's sermons or centered around vital community interests of the members of the congregation.

Research is essential to the development of meaningful program; and, if carefully conducted, studied, and used, it leads not only to improved program but to the satisfactory development of planning, coordination, and evaluation.

Coordination. Coordination is frequently and falsely placed in the planning process *following* the making of the congregation's plans. The best coordination takes place at many levels during the development of the plans of the congregation's life. For example:

- *Coordination at the planning group level*

  Whatever style of planning is used, coordination is essential for each group, taking into account the personnel, building, equipment, and financial resources available. For instance, the education committee or department may plan its leadership training responsibility. But whatever program it designs, it must take into account other programs of the congregation and what time, personnel, space, and financial resources are available.

- *Coordination by use of the congregational calendar*

  As plans are made and dates for the carrying out of projects, programs, and events become evident, they should be placed on a central church calendar. Conflicting dates will need to be adjusted. Changes in established dates should be made only by persons authorized to do so and in accordance with agreed-upon procedures.

- *Coordination at the intercommittee level*

  Such coordination may take place in two areas of intercommittee work: (1) it may be initiated and conducted between the committees or departments involved; (2) it may be accomplished at the church cabinet level. Again, it will be imperative to consider the availability of time, personnel, space, and financial resources. The church calendar, incorporating dates proposed by various planning groups, can be developed by the cabinet and approved by the congregation.[8]

- *Coordination at the church cabinet level*

  Such coordination is designed to bring together all program, projects, and events planned in the life of the congregation. It makes sure that the time, space, personnel, and financial resources available are capable of supporting all that is planned, and that all that is planned contributes to the congregation's mission.

- *Coordination at the general board level*

  Coordination by this group is not a recommended practice. The general board, or steering committee in some congregations, should be a legislative, not a coordinating, body. However, if the congregation desires to use the general board or a similar body for coordination, this will be effective as the congregation seeks to make it a viable instrument in this area of work.

Coordination is designed to make the most effective use of the congregation's resources. It will enable the congregation to focus its attention upon one or a few—never many—emphases at a given time. Coordination will enable the congregation to place its resources in a vital way in support of the major program thrusts it has chosen to use in response to God's mission.

Evaluation. Evaluation is essential. It provides the proper tone to program. Usually evaluation is employed after a program, project, or event has been concluded. However, it will be most effective if planned for at the inception of the program or built into the program.

8. See *Annual Planning Guide and Calendar* and *See-at-a-Glance Program Planning Calendar* (Indianapolis: National Church Program Coordinating Council).

A general evaluation session may be held midway through each program year by the staff and program leaders. This can provide the congregation with a reading of the effectiveness of program planned. It can also indicate where changes need to be made, or what program needs to be deleted, or whether a new program needs to be instituted.

An annual evaluation session for staff and program leaders will be useful in preparing for planning the next year's program. Results of the evaluation should be made known to the general board and congregation and serve as the basis for a service of celebration and/or achievement. Such a service can be held at the conclusion of a program year and at the beginning or launch of the new program year.

Evaluation is based upon clearly understood meanings of the congregation's response to God's mission. What does the congregation propose to do to make effective witness in terms of its response to God's mission? The setting forth of these proposals in *measurable and reasonably achievable* goals is imperative if evaluation is to be carried out by leaders; by committee, department, or task groups; or by program participants.

Measurable and reasonably achievable goals are essential to both sound program and evaluation. It is not difficult to make goals measurable when the results of the goals are stated statistically. For example, a goal of fifty-two hundred in church school attendance in a calendar year is measurable and easily subject to evaluation. This means the church school must average one hundred in attendance each Sunday. Whether or not the goal is reasonable depends upon the past record of the church school, the procedures designed for achieving added attendance, and the resource pool of population from which to draw new participants.

In dealing with qualitative rather than quantitative evaluation, the problem is quite different. For example, a congregation may seek to develop better communication with the community in order to make evident the Good News in the community. The goals must be stated in terms of desired outcomes. The following series of assumptions illustrates one way of stating the matter:

- Assumption that there is a felt gap between the congregation and community leaders
- Assumption that the gap is primarily in the area of social ethics
- Assumption that communication between the congregation and the community may be a basic problem (it might prove to be a problem of theology)
- Assumption that conversations may identify some things to be done to bridge the gap

It is possible to take these assumptions related to the hypothesis and develop appropriate planning as the guide to evaluation.

Evaluation, when carefully used, and when the congregation is ready to respond to the learning derived from it, can provide the following results for future planning and program:

- Establish success or failure of programs or events based upon their expected outcomes
- Establish those parts of programs or events that were useful or not useful in achieving the desired or expected outcomes
- Illuminate the possibility of correct or incorrect quality of desired outcomes
- Indicate new procedures or techniques that need to be used

- Indicate programs or events that need to be deleted from the congregation's response to God's mission
- Indicate adjustments needed in programs or events already in operation to sharpen the effectiveness of the congregation's response to God's mission

Physical Tools

Physical instrumentalities are materials, buildings, grounds, and equipment. Each congregation must choose what it deems appropriate for the achievement of its response to God's mission.

Guidance and study materials of many kinds are needed to make possible the introduction of the individual and the congregation to God's will and continued growth in understanding and acting upon that will.

Buildings may or may not be important to the congregation's response to God's mission. Most congregations have buildings, but some do not. The latter meet in homes or rented facilities. Some congregations carry out their work in shopping centers, social centers, on streets, on beaches, etc. One fact is becoming increasingly evident, namely, that for some of these congregations, buildings may be a hindrance to the fulfillment of mission as often as they are a help. Congregations need to evaluate what can be most helpfully achieved by their use. Perhaps congregations that determine they need buildings will find it most appropriate to build ones with multiple-use space. For example, they can have a sanctuary that can be used for worship, recreation, and fellowship rather than a sanctuary with the more permanent type of furnishings that make it impossible to use the room for little more than worship one hour (perhaps two hours) a week.

Equipment is essential and will be determined by the type of work in which the congregation engages. Equipment may include choir and ministerial robes, communion service, candelabra, lawn mowers, books, magazines, curriculum materials, projectors, furnaces, hearing aids, organs, etc. In any event, equipment should be of good quality, useful, and designed to take advantage of the best techniques available for its use. At the same time, it should be recognized that heavy expenditures for equipment may become a hindrance to adequate response of the congregation to God's mission.

Summary

Congregational response to God's mission requires careful use of many available tools. Leadership and the whole congregation working together will determine the best use of planning, research, coordination, and evaluation in relationship to the physical instrumentalities of program materials, buildings, and equipment in order to respond effectively to God's mission in the world.

7

Organizing the Congregation for Mission

Organization is a servant of mission, never its master. Organization should enable the congregation to make an effective response to its understanding of God's mission in the world. The members should discover within the congregation's organization the opportunity to make maximum use of their several abilities to serve both God and man. The congregation, in its corporate life, should be enabled to respond to God's mission by effective action and service to its own members and to the community and world in which it lives.

Congregational organization, like any other kind of organization, can become dangerous, if not destructive, to the life of the group. When the congregation—its minister(s), lay leaders, and other members—becomes so involved with organization that the purpose for which the organization exists is forgotten, then the life of the congregation is in danger of destruction.

The congregation will find it helpful to choose that form of organization best suited to its understanding of God's mission, capable of making effective response to that mission and making fullest use of the abilities and attitudes of its members.

The congregation will also find it helpful to view its organization as interim or transitory in character. Flexibility is of basic importance. Otherwise, the organization may become more important than either the mission or the response. As the congregation's understanding of God's mission expands and as its will and ability to respond in service change, it may become evident that the congregation's organization must change. Such change should not occur for the sake of novelty, but for justifiable reasons related to mission and service.

When organization becomes a set of rigid structures to be maintained, the congregation is equally in danger of destruction. A letter from a lay leader in one congregation asked, "Does a committee of the congregation have to meet because a meeting is scheduled, when the committee has nothing to do?" Such a question indicates that organization has become a rigid form to be followed and, therefore, as Paul said of the law, is "death itself." Of course, no committee should meet just because a meeting is scheduled! For that matter, no committee should exist just because the congregation has said there should be such a committee. Organization should be the enabler and carrier of the congregation's response to God's mission. This requires that meetings be held when needed and committees and task groups organized when there is work to be accomplished.

Each congregation should develop an organization that enables it to witness effectively to its accepted understanding of God's mission. This means that a congregation of a few members will need an organization different from that of a larger congregation; and a congregation involved in an inner-city response to God's mission may need an organization different from that of a congregation in a suburban or small-town situation. Varying types of organization should be used where needed, and accepted without prejudice. Paul, in the twelfth chapter of 1 Corinthians, gives wise counsel in this matter, when he says: "To each is given the manifestation of the Spirit for the common good.... For just as the body is one and has many members, and all the members of the body, though many, are one body, so it is with Christ.... For the body does not consist of one member but of many" (vv. 7, 12, 14).

In determining the kind of organization needed, a congregation should consider the arenas in which it can make its witness effective. This may be illustrated by the following design:

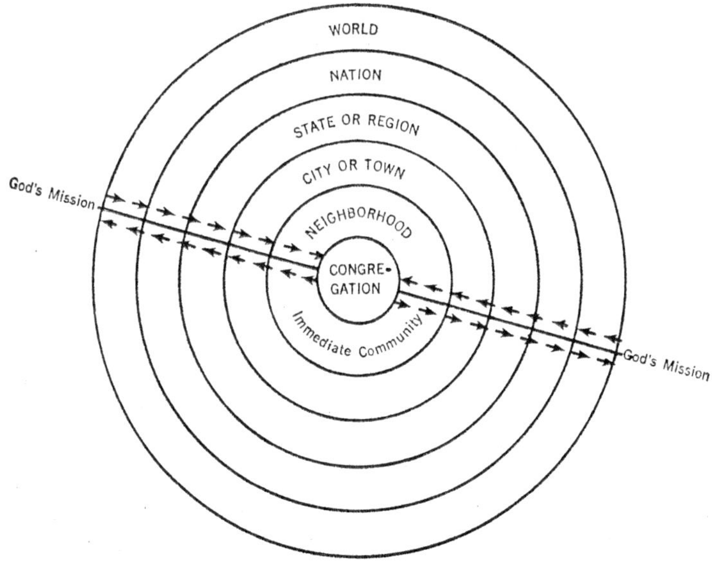

This design, which appears simple, has several implications. The line bisecting the concentric circles indicates that God's mission comes to the congregation both from God's revelation in the world and through Jesus Christ. The arrows on both sides of the bisecting line indicate that the congregation partakes of and responds to God's mission. The congregation is not a self-contained unit existing for its own internal purposes but is part of a larger whole in terms of church and the secular society.

The question that has to be answered is, *What kind of congregation can best make effective the congregation's response to God's mission?*

Before this question is considered, a word needs to be said concerning the kind of constituency that exists in today's congregation. Frequently, it can be described as being either past middle age and not involved in social action or under middle age and social-action centered. The former kind of constituency is made up of those who follow the more "traditional" understanding of the church, while the latter is more experimental and, in that sense, nontraditional. The fact is, most congregations are something of both. Sometimes there is dissent, if not friction. The result is that most congregations today are faced with certain internal problems which, while difficult, must be met to maximize the resources of all in response to God's mission. New congregations may determine their direction more easily, but the traditional and the nontraditional must be kept together in the spirit of love and witness.

In preparation for consideration of various patterns of suggested organization, it may be helpful to review chapter 5, "Characteristics of the Congregation as Church," and chapter 6, "Tools for the Congregation." Theological characteristics of the congregation are identified as mission, love, and servanthood. Applied theological characteristics are identified as nurture and action. Nurture and action are detailed as follows:

Nurture	*Action*
Evangelism and Churchmanship	Social Involvement
Education	Stewardship
Worship	Outreach

The theological and applied theological characteristics of the congregation are resources for responding to God's mission. These resources are augmented by some basic organization of the church evidenced as early as New Testament times, namely, ministers (bishops), elders, deacons, and deaconesses. The role of the minister will be dealt with in chapter 8. The roles of elders, deacons, and deaconesses have changed through the years. Today, with new roles, they can provide the important resource of specially equipped persons for the effective witness and service of the congregation. As a matter of fact, ministers, elders, deacons, and deaconesses form an important "corps" of leaders in every congregation.

According to the Scriptures, elders are to become spiritual leaders of the congregation. All too frequently, however, they are the trustees of the congregation's property and concerned primarily with holding title to and maintaining that property. To achieve their intended role, elders should steep themselves in knowledge of the Scriptures and in Christian acts that give evidence of their spiritual maturity. They can then become a vital spiritual resource along with the minister(s) in conducting the priestly and pastoral work of the church. Acting as consultative adviser to the minister(s), calling on the ill, serving the poor, and aiding in the fellowship and evangelism calling are all important aspects of the work of elders. Another area of importance for elders, and one which is all too frequently overlooked in many congregations, is that of recruitment and guidance of individuals in the congregation who are interested in a church vocation.

Deacons and deaconesses can be an aid to the minister(s) and elders of the congregation in serving the needs of the fellowship and the community.

The minister(s), elders, deacons, and deaconesses are persons specially prepared to help the congregation in developing and making effective its witness and service.

The following plans for congregational organization are offered not as *the* organization for any specific congregation but as suggestions from which any congregation can develop its own organization. *The plans suggested on these pages are samples of those presently operating in one or more congregations of the Christian Church (Disciples of Christ) in the United States and Canada.*

PLAN I. CONGREGATIONAL ORGANIZATION

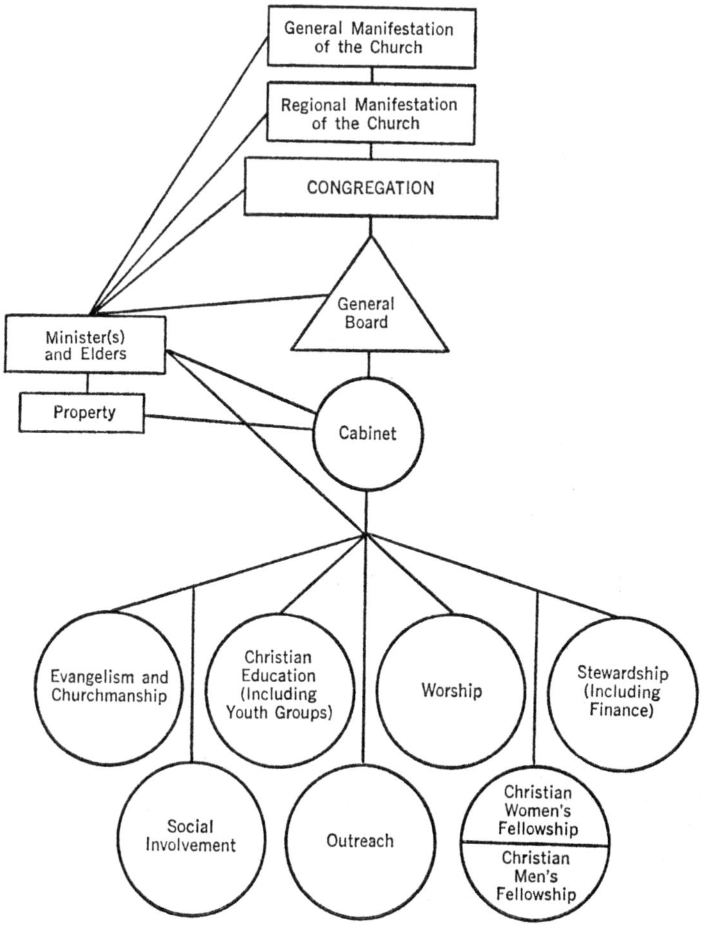

PLAN II. CONGREGATIONAL ORGANIZATION

ASSIGNMENTS AND RELATIONSHIPS IN FUNCTIONAL ORGANIZATION

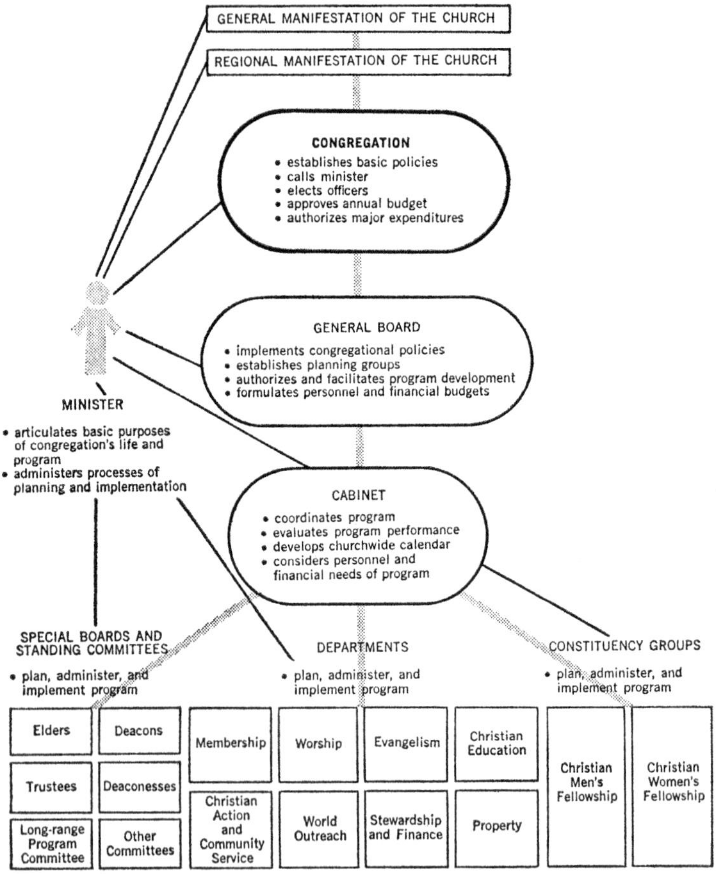

The above chart is adapted from Dale W. Medearis, **The Congregation Plans for Action,** Church Program Guidance Manuals (Indianapolis: National Church Program Coordinating Council, 1966), p. 28.

PLAN III. CONGREGATIONAL ORGANIZATION

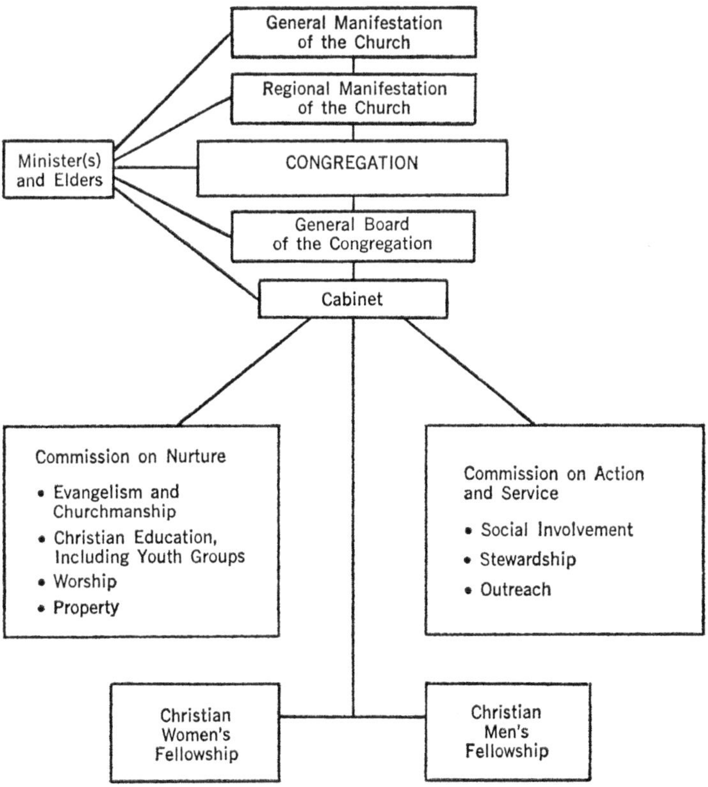

PLAN IV. CONGREGATIONAL ORGANIZATION

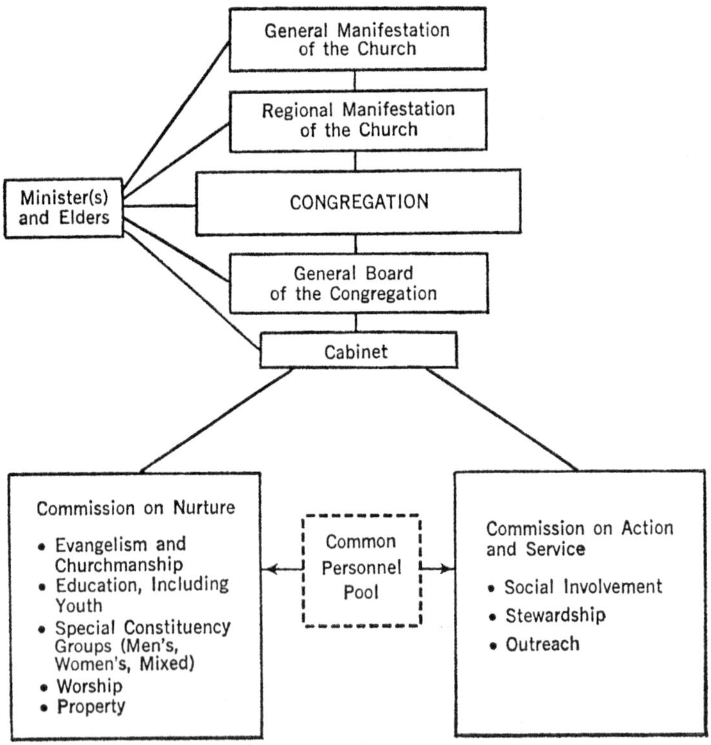

PLAN V. CONGREGATIONAL ORGANIZATION

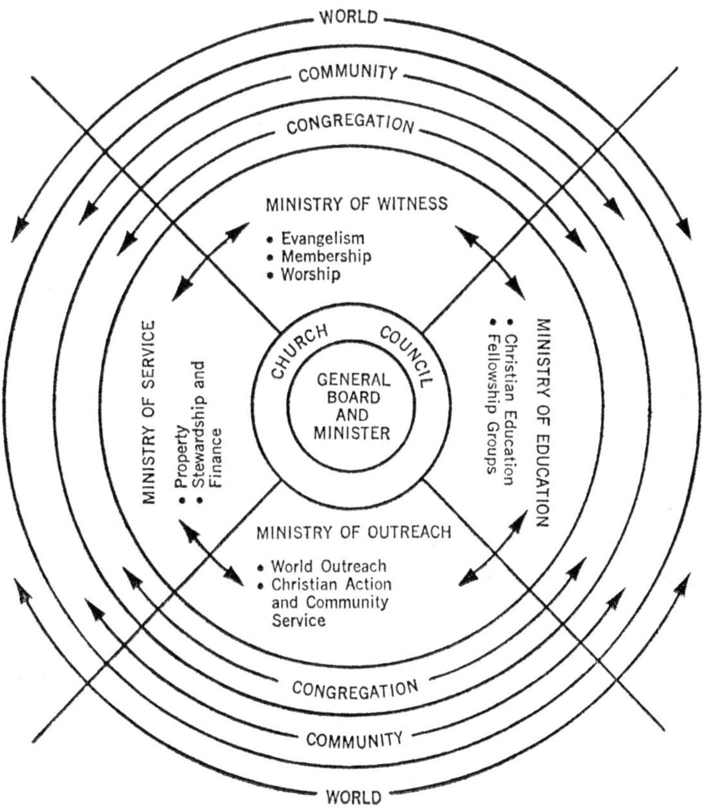

Plan I provides for the congregation to utilize the characteristics of the congregation as church (see chapter 5) as the basis for its organization. It also provides for the general board and cabinet of the congregation.

The basic responsibilities of the general board are to legislate, establish policies, oversee contracts, and authorize budgets and other matters to be referred to the congregation for action.

The membership of the board, including the number of members, should be established by the congregation either in articles of operation or in a constitution and bylaws. In some congregations the general board is composed of the elders, deacons, and deaconesses. In others, the general board is elected at large and may or may not include elders, deacons, and deaconesses. In any event, adequate representation of women and youth should be included in the general board membership.

The cabinet consists of the heads of the committees, departments or commissions, and fellowships of the congregation. Its purpose is to coordinate their plans and work. The cabinet is not a legislative but an advisory body to both the general board and the minister(s).

Major committees and the Christian Women's Fellowship and the Christian Men's Fellowship will be dealt with in Part III of this book. The work of the constituency groups of the congregation—youth groups, Christian Women's Fellowship, and Christian Men's Fellowship—should be related to the committees and departments or commissions indicated in Plan I.

In Plan I, social involvement and overseas witness can be combined, thereby making one less committee.

Plan II is generally known as Functional Organization and is widely used by congregations of the Disciples of Christ.

Plan III shows the relationship of the congregation to the regional (state/area) and general (national and international) manifestations of the church (see Appendix B).

Plan III reduces the number of committees to two commissions—a commission on nurture, with four task groups under it, and a commission on action and service, with three task groups. It should be noted, however, that the use of task groups can be developed in any form of organization. A task group is defined as "a small group designed to accomplish a specific task within a limited time." In light of this definition, the above are not precisely task groups. Task groups as used today are more commonly understood as subcommittees. Consequently, Plan III can be implemented with task groups, if they are understood as subcommittees of the commissions.

Plan IV differs from Plan III in that each of the two commissions is responsible for all the items listed, and the *personnel of each commission is used to plan and conduct the work of the respective commission.* Specific programs, projects, and events related to each commission's work are carried out by task groups designed to accomplish a specific task within a limited span of time. The result is an organization that is highly flexible and capable of being operated by a minimum number of people. Consequently, Plan IV may be an option for small congregations. Larger congregations can use the resources of many persons—and should do so—in response to God's mission in the world.

It should be pointed out, however, that the smaller congregation has both the opportunity and responsibility to be related to the regional and general manifestations of the church.

Plan V indicates a congregation's response to God's mission in terms of witness/action to the congregation, community, and world. The ministries of the congregation are identified as evangelism, membership, worship, etc. They are coordinated through the church council and legislated through the general board of the congregation. The style of work is that of task groups working on specific projects. This plan provides for maximum flexibility and mobility of the congregation to meet the rapidly changing needs in the congregation, community, and world.

Selecting an Organizational Pattern for Use by the Congregation

The congregation should select the organizational pattern that best enables it to respond to God's mission. Some of the questions to be answered in developing the organization for use by the congregation are:

- Which organization enables the congregation to respond most effectively to God's mission?
- Which organization provides the opportunity for flexibility in meeting the rapidly changing issues confronting the congregation?
- Which organization provides the opportunity for the congregation faithfully to express its special responsibility as given in chapter 5, "Characteristics of the Congregation as Church"?
- Which organization most adequately uses the personnel potential of the congregation?
- Which organization can best be administered in light of the congregation's experience and attitude toward democratic procedures?

A final word in the form of a reminder needs to be said about organization. Each congregation needs to develop the type of organization that is most useful to its response to God's mission. The congregation needs to understand that organization is only the beginning. The objective of organization is to enable the congregation to respond effectively to God's mission and to participate in the reconciling ministry of Jesus Christ.

Summary

The congregation needs flexible and mobile organization in order to meet human need in a rapidly changing world. Five suggested patterns of organization have been presented, with the understanding that each congregation must develop that organization and style of operation best suited to its desired response to God's mission.

8

The Minister and Laity in Mission

Every day brings something new. Wildest dreams become fact. The world is changing, changing—and clergy and laity are going to be tried to the extreme by the challenges to come.

The expanding body of scientific knowledge seems in some quarters to make the role of religion uncertain, if not unnecessary. It should be understood that the mood of science at the beginning of the decade of the seventies is not that of the forties. When atom bombs were dropped on Hiroshima and Nagasaki, men of science took the position that they were not responsible for the use of their discoveries. In the intervening years many scientists have become deeply concerned about the value systems and the questions of ethics related to their discoveries. Now they are seeking new understandings of the relationship between the metaphysical and physical worlds. Some of them say quite openly that they want the help of religion in understanding the meanings of value systems and ethics in life as related to religion. The church and the world of religion are being challenged to find new meanings and bridges of understanding between science and religion, and to render service to the people of science.

Another exciting challenge to the church in the latter part of the twentieth century is that of development in the Third

World. The needs of the poverty-stricken for education, economic justice, and tools for self-help are common knowledge. Not since the renewal of the church by Francis of Assisi and his ministry to the poor has the church faced such an immense opportunity to bear witness to humanity and serve it in response to God's mission in the world.

Personal spiritual renewal is an additional challenge. One example of personal spiritual renewal is the rediscovery of the meaning of fellowship (koinonia). Such renewal can provide the congregation with an increasing number of persons who, discovering anew the meaning of the Good News, are willing to commit themselves to applying that discovery in the life of the congregation and the community. The result of such discovery and application may be a congregation of fewer members, but with increasingly effective response to God's mission.

The many challenges before the church—in addition to those noted above—may properly include the earth itself (air, water, animals, etc.), the human body (health, drugs, age, reproduction, etc.), the generation gap, the present generation reaching maturity, and international peace.

These challenges, and others, have caused scholars to study the Scriptures in new depth, with the result that the rich meanings of the Bible are being brought into new focus as man seeks to set right the human relationships in the world. One of the rich meanings becoming increasingly evident is a renewed understanding of what it means to be called "the people of God" *(laos)*.

The concept of "the people of God" is based upon God's covenant with Abraham (Gen. 12, 17) and reaffirmed by the Christ, when he said, "I am the good shepherd; I know my own and my own know me" (John 10:14). The covenant relationship finds further support in many other references, among which are these:

> " ... for he will save his people [*laos*] from their sins" (Matt. 1:21).
>
> "the people [*laos*] who sat in darkness
> have been a great light,
> and for those who sat in the region
> and shadow of death
> light has dawned" (Matt. 4:16).
>
> "Once you were no people [*laos*] but now you are God's people; once you had not received mercy but now you have received mercy" (1 Peter 2:10).

In New Testament times and the life of the early church, "the people of God" were understood to be both ministers (bishops) and laity. In the twentieth century the concept of "the people of God" has fallen into disuse with the rise of the clergy (ministers) as the professional leaders and the laity as the nonprofessional members of the congregation. The "people of God" are the whole membership of the church, both professional clergy and nonprofessional lay members. However, though we must not forget the concept of "the people of God," for the purpose of these pages the terms *clergy* and *minister* will refer to the professional leadership of the church and the term *laity* will refer to the nonprofessional members of the church.

The Minister in Mission

Ministers are, for the most part, highly trained for their profession. Educational institutions responsible for the training of the clergy are making clear the professional character of the clergy in terms of the degrees granted for three or four years of graduate study in addition to the four years of study for the B.A. degree. It should be noted that the academic training of the clergy is equivalent to or in excess of that needed for teaching, law, and most other professions with the exception of the medical profession. In addition, the minister, like the teacher, lawyer, and doctor, will find it necessary to engage in continuing educational experiences at regular intervals throughout his career if he chooses to be knowledgeable and effective.

The minister has many responsibilities. In his book, James D. Glasse refers to the various roles of the minister described by Samuel Blizzard. Five of these are preacher, priest, teacher, organizer, and administrator.[1] To this list can be added prophet.

The role of the minister as *preacher* is dependent upon the professional qualities that he brings to his office. Preaching is based upon the ability of the minister to communicate in plain language the eternal truths of God applied to the human situation. The minister needs freedom as a preacher, and this freedom must be provided and maintained by the laity of the congregation. Gentle firmness must be used by the minister in "rightly handling" the truth of God in making apparent the love of God. Preaching requires a scholarly knowledge and use of the Scriptures, literature, history, and the needs of humanity. The congregation will find it beneficial to support the minister in a regimen of study reduced to a schedule of daily reading and meditation.

While freedom for the preacher is necessary, it is also becoming increasingly necessary that he have a vital openness to the laity. Some regular form of providing the laity with the opportunity to discuss and question the minister about his preaching is desirable. Such openness requires that he have a sense of inner security based upon careful study and abiding spiritual development and the evident acceptance and support of the congregation. If these qualities abide, then the

1. James D. Glasse, *Profession: Minister* (New York: Abingdon Press, 1968), p. 58, citing Samuel W. Blizzard, "The Minister's Dilemma," *The Christian Century* (April 25, 1956), pp. 508–10.

minister will not see questions and discussion as a threat to him personally but as the laity's searching for new truth in its response to God's mission.

The role of the minister as *priest* is ancient and imperative. In performance of his priestly office, the minister realizes that he is truly a servant of God dispensing hope and assurance that are not his own. As a priest, the minister, on behalf of the congregation, comforts the ill and dying, counsels the distressed, and provides assurance of hope for the present and the future. He is the transmitter of the sacraments of the church, thereby providing the historical continuity of the covenant of God and the reality of God's love expressed through the crucifixion and resurrection of his Son, Jesus Christ.

Counseling has become an increasingly important part of the work of many ministers. When adequate training makes this kind of ministry possible, it is valid; but care must be exercised so that the minister recognizes his limitations and stands ready to call professional help at the first sign of the need of such assistance. Moreover, counseling is not so much the manipulation of the techniques of psychological inquiry or even of psychological analysis. Counseling is, at its best, a means of providing the minister with a way of helping the individual to understand what God is doing in the world and the life of the individual.

The congregation will be strengthened through the role of the minister as *prophet,* which will be essential to the congregation's relevance in the world. Leslie Dewart, professor of the Institute of Christian Thought, St. Michael's College, Toronto, Canada, has observed that many ministers engage in "homiletical prophecy," which is preaching *at* the congregation. Professor Dewart goes on to point out that the church is in need of the kind of prophecy that plans for the options of the future so that when the future is realized the needed options are available. For one thing, this means discerning the future and planning for it.

Another aspect of meaningful prophecy, other than planning for it, is that of involvement in the life of humanity. In a way, this is prophecy in action. It is prophecy by example. Prophecy is the speaking, explaining, and declaring in deed the understood truth of God. The minister, as the good prophet, inspires the congregation to become participants in the mission of God.

The role of the minister as *teacher* is vital to any renewal of the professional quality of the minister and to the renewal of the life of the congregation. The New Testament indicates that the Master did not refuse the title "rabbi." In Jesus' world, the rabbi was a teacher. Jesus went from place to place, teaching. He was the master teacher. It is appropriate, therefore, that the minister accept the task of being the master teacher in the congregation. This does not mean he does all the teaching. It does mean that he is at the center of the teaching-learning ministry of the congregation. It means that he does the basic and essential teaching in the training of the leadership of the congregation, especially in the areas of theological training and biblical studies. In this connection, it is important to note the usefulness of the Christian Life Curriculum, built upon the rediscovery of the ancient role of the minister as the master teacher.

The role of the minister as *organizer and administrator* is basic to his and the congregation's response to God's mission in the world. The minister is called to be the chief administrator of the congregation as much as he is called to any other task. The congregation's response to God's mission is to be dealt with in all the roles of the minister, but if he fails to enable the congregation to organize and to plan program and then administer that organization and planned program, both he and the congregation will fail to respond adequately to God's mission.

As stated in *The Minister and the Christian Life Curriculum*:

The minister is the general administrator of the congregation. In this role he is the administrator of the congregation's program of which the church's educational program is a part. In general, the minister, as administrator, is responsible for the following [from *The Congregation Plans for Action,* Medearis]:

- articulation of the basic purposes of the congregation's life and program
- administration of the processes of planning and implementation
- recruitment and development of leaders
- development of a creative attitude toward tension and conflict

The minister's administrative role does not imply taking responsibility from the laity. To the contrary, the minister, as general administrator of the congregation, is responsible for helping the laity develop an effective program of action in the life and witness of the congregation.

The minister partly fulfills his function as general administrator within the organizational structure of the congregation through its various boards, departments, etc. The organizational structure varies from one congregation to another.[2]

Program-Planning and Administrative Flow

It is trite but true to say that congregations are not alike. Many group themselves along lines of similarity, but even then they tend to group themselves according to whether they have the "functional" plan of organization and procedures (or close variations), or follow an earlier type of organization. Others are beginning to experiment with organization along fellowship group lines or some other organizing principle. Following are three charts that help visualize the pro-

2. Kenneth A. Kuntz, *The Minister and the Christian Life Curriculum* (St. Louis: Christian Board of Publication, 1968), p. 23. Used by permission.

cesses involved in program-planning and administration for *functionally organized, nonfunctionally organized,* and *new* congregations.[3]

The Functionally Organized Congregation

In brief, this shows the processes involved in program-planning and administration, from the time of the decision to begin planning to the time plans are actually put into action.

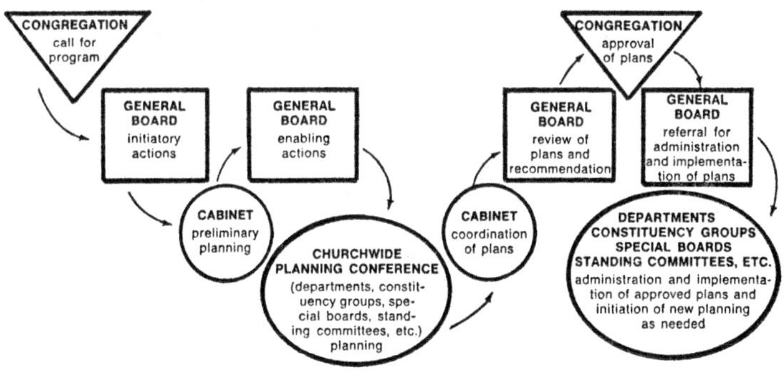

The Small Congregation

Many small congregations are rich in resources for program-planning and administration. All the small congregation needs to do is follow the above general plan, but make assignments to individuals instead of to groups, and depend on the general board or congregation in session to do many of the things indicated for the cabinet, board, and planning conference.

The Nonfunctionally Organized Congregation

Program-planning may begin by the general board's taking

3. This paragraph and the material below and on the following page are adapted from Dale W. Medearis, *The Congregation Plans for Action,* Church Program Guidance Manuals (Indianapolis: National Church Program Coordinating Council, 1966), pp. 24–25.

the matter under consideration and deciding to go through the necessary planning steps. The board itself, or a specifically appointed committee, needs to do the preliminary planning, as does the board in the functionally organized congregation. After preliminary planning, a special meeting of the most responsible leaders of the congregation should be convened as a planning conference. When the conference is over, the board should coordinate the plans and develop a calendar for the year to serve as a guide in the implementation. The board should then refer the plans to the congregation for action and take the necessary steps throughout the year to get the plans into operation.

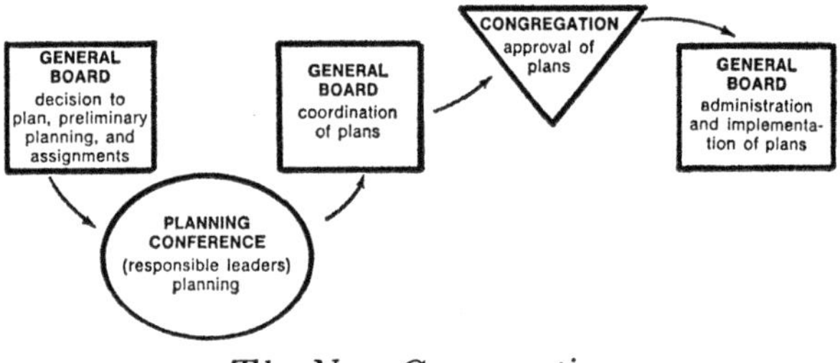

The New Congregation

Temporary organization is the mode. Many new congregations have steering committees rather than general boards and convene the congregation in a "town meeting" for most of the business and policy decisions. With this kind of organization, quite adequate planning can go forward using the resources that any other kind of congregation would use.

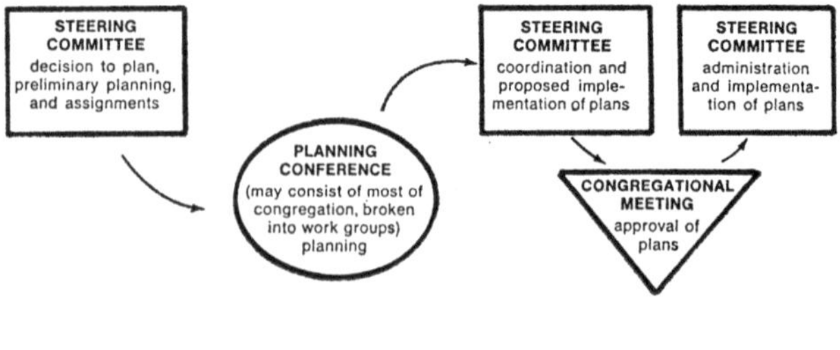

Administrator is the one role of the minister least appreciated by many ministers and some congregations, yet it holds great opportunity for achievement in witness and service. Administration, among other things, is making evident the characteristics of the congregation as church (chapter 5). Administration is making possible the orderly use of the resources, personnel, and material of the congregation (chapter 6). Administration is allowing the laity to be in the forefront of action. In this role the minister supports the laity in training, organization, and administration.

An additional responsibility of the minister is to participate in the district, regional, general, and ecumenical work of the church, and often to give leadership in such work. Congregations can aid in making this kind of service possible by indicating their willingness for ministers to accept and serve in positions of responsible leadership in community service and in the regional, general, and ecumenical manifestations of the church. This would provide the congregation with increasingly beneficial leadership because of the experiences of the minister. It is possible, also, that use of such leadership by regional, general, and ecumenical offices would make possible more useful deployment of their present staffs or even a decrease in their staffs.

Congregations will do well to recognize the quality of ministerial leadership provided. It needs to be remembered that, in a real sense, congregations employ ministers. In this connection, certain things are in order, such as the following suggestions from an ex-pastor:

Have a definite *job description* for the minister.

• • •

Treat him as a leader—not a handmaid.

• • •

Allow the minister to lead a life separate from church if he so desires.

• • •

A man's home is his *privacy*. Do not regulate this life.

• • •

Congregations ought to at least *meet minimum personnel policies* and practices adhered to in the business world, in treatment of their professional leadership.[4]

The Laity in Mission

The decade of the 1960s witnessed the rising awareness of the importance of the laity and the intensification of the need for its involvement in the whole life of the congregation and other manifestations of the church. The laity in the 1960s brought a new element to the life of the church in that it sought to turn the church outward to the world. Georgia Harkness, in *The Church and Its Laity,* has this to say:

> ... these enterprises have a common center and point of reference. This center is God's yearning concern for the whole world and His supreme gift of Jesus Christ for the salvation and upbuilding of men. This concern includes all persons in all lands and cultures and—what is more commonly overlooked—in all aspects of their lives.[5]

Characteristics of the increased involvement of the laity in response to God's mission in the world may be understood in the following:

- New awareness of the meaning of laity
- New understanding of the meaning of church
- New involvement in the world

4. Gerald J. Jud, Edgar W. Mills, Jr., and Genevieve Walters Burch, *Ex-Pastors: Why Men Leave the Parish Ministry* (Philadelphia: United Church Press, 1970), p. 6.

5. (New York: Abingdon Press, 1962), pp. 155–56.

The first half of the twentieth century saw the laity, in many instances, exercising the same kind of power in the church as it did in business and politics, leaving its self-renewal to the professional leadership of the clergy. New philosophies and theologies emerged following the Second World War, and the laity rapidly began to see itself in new roles that would have meaning for both the congregation and the world.

The result of new awareness of the meaning of laity is an increasingly productive life-style in which the men, women, and youth of the church are expressing their faith through action in the field of Christian ethics. Consequently, faith is being expressed in terms of involvement in political enterprises, social-welfare services, reconciliation between ethnic and racial groups, and the struggle for peace.

The congregation—indeed, the whole church—is responding to the impact of the laity's new self-awareness. For instance, general boards of congregations, once dominated by men, are increasingly including women and youth in their memberships. This is encouraged not because women and youth should be represented as women and youth, but because they have abilities, associations, and expertise of their own without which the church cannot adequately respond to God's mission in the world.

Laymen have found new involvement in the world. The world belongs to them because that is where they live, work, and engage in daily activities. Therefore, they are increasingly expressing their understandings of faith discovered in the congregation and practiced in their daily lives. The home and the community with its many enterprises in the social, political, and economic arenas of life are becoming the setting for the witness of the people of faith.

Laymen who once were willing to attend the committee meetings of the congregation, which, for the most part, were directed to the maintenance of the internal life of the congregation, are no longer content with such activity. They are not unwilling to attend committee, group, or task force meetings, but they want to see the relevance of these meetings for the community. They want to see the hungry fed, the naked clothed, the homeless provided shelter, and the sick healed. The laity is struggling to make this a world of peace, a world where dignity of the individual is not desecrated by the ambitions and avarice of others and where the gospel teachings, so long orally expressed, are given substance in action.

The laity has gained new understandings of the meaning of the gospel and the church of Jesus Christ. For generations the church has taught the meaning of love and its primacy in the gospel. Achieving peace has been a central purpose of the church. Christ has been identified as the Prince of Peace. The success of this teaching and purpose is evident as laymen now take seriously their understandings of both love and peace. While this should be a matter of great satisfaction to the church, the fact is that this new awareness of the meaning of the gospel is disturbing the church. Ironically, the success of the church at this point is also contributing to the intense conflict that occurs in the church when some young people take these teachings seriously. The challenge before the church—and especially each congregation—is to increase its effective teaching and celebrate the involvement of the laity both in the church and in the world.

New Understandings of the Gospel

The increase of effective teaching of the gospel depends upon three specific needs:

- New understandings of the gospel
- New commitments to gospel meanings
- New engagements in God's mission in the world

The Good News of the Scriptures has been used as the basis for individual and corporate spiritual development, and for expression of Christian action in the world. Both purposes are important to the full Christian life, but the one is not a substitute for the other.

Spiritual renewal, which is a daily need for every person and group, is one of the primary objectives in the use of the Scriptures. To move beyond the use of the Scriptures for personal and group devotions to such renewal is to grasp the broad and deeper meanings. For example, Paul wrote to the Corinthians about the problems of the young church struggling to identify both the Good News and the world in which it lived while not allowing the church to be overcome by the world. He wrote to the Romans to share with them the meaning of the message of Christ and to prepare them for his forthcoming visit. These letters, and many others of the New Testament, were not written as a record of personal devotional life, but as direct communication from restless men acting out God's mission. Paul was, as Peter wrote, "prepared to make a defense to any one who calls you to account for the hope that is in you ... " (1 Peter 3:15).

The laity, to fulfill its response to God's mission, must study the Scriptures deeply in order to understand the nature and meaning of its response. In addition, the laity must come to see God revealing himself and the nature of his mission in the form of human need and in terms of the issues of a world in need.

The gospel calls the laity to understand that God speaks through human need as well as through the words of the Scriptures. The "crossing point" theory of the Christian Life Curriculum is a case in point. A "crossing point" is experienced when man's persistent life needs are intersected by the revelation of God in Jesus Christ. This "crossing point" experience provides the opportunity for the discovery of new life meanings and practices.

For example, the parable of the Good Samaritan is frequently understood in terms of the needs of the victim of the robbers and the apparently appropriate response of the Samaritan to these needs. But, what of the needs of the others in this parable? The robbers had needs all too easily overlooked. They were slaves of their own life values expressed in living off the labors of others. The priest and the Levite had unmet needs in the form of their slavery to a system of religion that isolated them from human need. And, what of the Samaritan? Could it be that he had need to serve others for his own self-identity and satisfaction?

To return to the victim, it is barely possible that he had unanswered needs even before the robbery. It could be that he was going to Jericho for a vacation and to enjoy the warm waters of the salt sea. He had hoarded his money and, carrying with him the burden of this unshared wealth, fell victim to robbers.

The point is, all have needs of one kind or another. Deep study of the Scriptures and the world in which we live day by day opens broad new vistas of understanding.

Laymen, to be effective in the congregation and the world, must engage in study such as that presently provided in special Bible studies, retreats, or lay schools of theology. Equally important is a study of their community and world. They should conduct their studies with one question in mind: What action in the world is required of my understanding of the gospel?

The answer to this question takes many forms. For example, four laymen in the First Christian Church in Fort Madison, Iowa, took seriously the scripture "I was in prison and you came to me" and developed a program of working with those in the state penitentiary located in that city.

They formed an "inmate-outmate" discussion group under the guidance of the chaplain and with approval of the warden. The purpose of the program is "to provide a religious therapy situation in which the members of the groups can express and examine their ideas and feelings about living in today's world."[6]

Another response is given by the Covenant Players, organized by Charles Tanner, of Los Angeles, California. The Players have nine traveling groups in various parts of the United States composed of laity and a few ministers and theological students. They seek to stimulate people to think about what they believe, and to challenge them to live the way they believe.

New commitments to gospel meanings require that the individual and the group face up to and deal with such issues as the following:

- Change in individual and group life
- Love as revealed in the life of Christ as the norm for human conduct and involvement
- Involvement in the struggle for peace, human dignity, and reconciliation among all men
- Development of spiritual disciplines of study and acceptance of project assignments
- Development of prayer practices related to vocational pursuits
- "Adoption" of strangers in the community
- "Adoption" of a person in a rest home or an older person living alone, etc.

6. Sherburne L. Ray, "Iowa Laymen Serve in Prison," *The Christian* (August 25, 1968), p. 24.

Change in Response to Gospel Meanings

Change seems to be one of the most difficult problems with which the congregation has to deal.

Psychologically, man seems to shrink from change because it forces him to deal with the future, which is always partially unknown and uncertain, or with present tensions, which cause conflict. It seems more comfortable and secure to try to stay where he is and to remain as he is. Nevertheless, change is at the heart of the gospel. Paul declares that we are to become "new creations" in Jesus Christ. Christ makes it clear that we are to become changed persons when he calls us to repentance and forgiveness sealed in the act of baptism and demonstrated regularly in the service of communion.

Change is an essential characteristic of everyday life. It is sometimes dramatic or traumatic, for example, at the birth of a child or at death, which has been described as "the end where all ends meet before the great beginning." Change also happens at the spiritual birth of a person, as exhibited by John Wesley at Aldersgate. More often, however, change is gradual and not so evident to the person or group being changed.

The involvement of the laity in mission requires dealing with change in an open and dynamic manner. Although this will not be easy for either the individual or the congregation, without it the status quo will sap the congregation of vitality and movement into the future.

Change is something common to all individuals and groups, and it must be dealt with as one of the norms of life. Acceptance of this fact is the first step in moving toward commitments to newly discovered gospel meanings.

The second step in making new commitments to gospel meanings is accepting love as revealed in the life of the Christ as the norm of human conduct and involvement. This means the acceptance of other individuals as persons and fulfilling faithfully the instructions of Christ when he said, "love one another as I have loved you."

Referring to the congregation as a fellowship or community of Christ means that the people have committed themselves to being joined together and to staying together. While there may be certain circumstances in which fellowship becomes strained or broken, the norm of love always keeps open the doors of reconciliation and suffers all things to keep from breaking fellowship.

The third step in making new commitments is to plan for dealing with controversial issues in both the individual and corporate life of the congregation. Some congregations try never to allow any expression of conflict, believing that thereby they have escaped the bumps that come with confronting conflict. Of course, such congregations are really dead and do not realize that it is by the sparks of flint against steel that new fires are made.

Dealing with conflict as a part of controversial issues requires providing the proper climate and means. The climate in which conflict can be satisfactorily dealt with is one of Christian love and the assurance that all issues will be faced openly and honestly. The search for God's will and its truth, and the willingness to discipline life to be committed to such truth, are important motivating forces in dealing with conflict.

Providing the means for dealing with conflict cannot be a spur-of-the-moment procedure. It requires an understanding of what conflict is.[7] Further, the congregation will find it helpful to have open discussions in forum style where all are heard and none threatened, and where individuals constantly attempt to arrive at decisions without prejudice

7. Robert Lee and Russell Galloway, *The Schizophrenic Church: Conflict over Community Organization* (Philadelphia: Westminster Press, 1969), pp. 165–82. (This reference is to chapter 9; however, study of the entire book is recommended.)

against the parties involved. Recognition of honest differences is essential in dealing with conflict. The readiness to admit error or to accept newly discovered truth is to be matched with the spirit of humility on the part of those who may be involved in conflict.

The capacity to accept others' behavior even though it is different from ours—even from that of the majority of the congregation—is essential in dealing with conflict. The capacity to face renewed challenges to positions that have been developed is necessary if solutions to conflict are not to become rigid, denying further search for truth, which may move to still further change. This is the ability to continue to love one another, whether winning or losing an argument.

Commitment to gospel meanings requires the laity to accept love as the basis for human conduct and involvement. It means seeing the congregation as the "family of God" and dealing with its day-to-day life. Jesus instructed his followers to "love your neighbor as yourself." Love of self requires self-understanding and self-acceptance. It means knowing whose, who, and what we are. It means knowing our human abilities and weaknesses. It means understanding that we can change, learn, and develop new abilities. When the individual discovers that these things are possible for himself, then he is at the threshold of loving his neighbor. Love means jointly learning, discovering, and growing together into new persons. This is the kind of love that opens human life to the fullness of its humanness and to the fullness of God's action in and through that life.

The laity should be involved in the struggle for personal peace and world peace. Following are some examples of what is happening in various communities:

- A group of laymen holds a weekly counseling service in an office in a shopping center.

- Youth participate in a march for peace in their city and in the nation's capital and give time to teaching retarded children.
- Women and men serve on community, state, and national committees dealing with equal employment opportunities, housing projects, equal education opportunity movements, and other similar works.[8]

Men and women not only serve on committees for better housing, but they assist in the actual renewal of houses to provide better housing in the inner city. It is in such work that the laity has turned what it has discovered in the church's teaching to the needs of its fellowmen in the world. Such work leads beyond the struggle for peace to the struggle for human dignity. Laymen are involved in reconciliation among all men. This is achieved not so much with words as with deeds. One group known as FISH responds to calls of people who are in need of all kinds of help, from transportation to a doctor's office or to the hospital, to finding a place to live or a job.

The laity is taking seriously new gospel meanings and committing itself to those new meanings. The church should rejoice in this and celebrate with thanksgiving that there are increasing numbers of men, women, and youth who are responding to God's mission in the world. Unfortunately, there are congregations that are afraid to venture into these new kinds of expression. The future will not be easy for any congregation and it will be less than certain; but it remains only for those congregations which dare new adventures to discover the benefit and joy of spiritual renewal that can bring renewal to the community and the world.

Let the voice of the laity be unfettered in the church. See

8. There are many illustrations of this type of involvement. Some may be found in the following book: Rüdiger Reitz, *The Church in Experiment* (New York: Abingdon Press, 1969).

to it that the men, women, and youth of the laity are the planners and decision makers and implementers of the congregation's response to God's mission. Let them be the officers of the congregation. Let them express their abilities and fulfill their newly discovered commitments to gospel meanings. Failures there may be, but without this freedom there will be no successes.

Summary

The minister and laity are essential to the congregation's response to God's mission. They both must be dedicated to mission and their joint responsibility to the world. Recognizing the professional contribution of the minister and the equally important contribution of the laity is essential to the renewal of the congregation and the work of God revealed through Jesus Christ in the world.

PART III

Congregations of the Christian Church (Disciples of Christ) in Mission Action

9

Mission Action Through Evangelism

Evangelism as described in chapter 5 is the proclamation of the evangel (Good News) of God and the invitation to all individuals to respond to his mission. Response involves repentance, confession, and dedication to Christian service in the world.

The word *evangelism* is composed of the root *evangel,* meaning the Good News, and the action suffix *ism.* Evangelism is a word conveying the image of a message actively proclaimed and affecting the life-style of the hearing-seeing receiver of the proclamation. Evangelism is a word of movement and action.

Evangelism is an essential characteristic of the Christian life. The prophetic call to repentance in the Old Testament and the preaching of John the Baptist in the wilderness bear testimony to the urgency of evangelism in the life of man. The life and message of Christ lend added weight to the centrality of evangelism to even the congregation.

The crucial need for evangelism in the life of the church

has been accepted in all ages of church history. At the beginning of the 1970s, however, there is probably no area more fraught with uncertainty and debate than that of evangelism. The debate has been shaped by many factors, especially those of the late 1950s. Some of the factors that have sharpened the debate are:

- The life-style of the congregation. In some cases, the congregation was thought of as a refuge from the world and, in others, the fellowship of renewal and preparation for Christian service in the world.
- The influence of Robinson's *Honest to God,* in which the God of "the out there" was challenged and awareness of God in man and his world was emphasized.
- Harvey Cox's *Secular City,* another expression of existential thought, which challenged man to turn away from secularism to accept God manifesting himself in the whole secular life of man in his cities.
- The rising awareness of the awful human need in the world—especially in the Third World—an awareness that was translated by a new breed of sociologists into challenges to the church in terms of both structure and message.

The result has been a crisis in the church identified by some as a "crisis of faith."

The "crisis of faith" that seems to be emerging in the 1970s involves searching for the abiding revelation of God through Jesus Christ in the world, the response of man to massive human need in the world, and the opportunity of celebrating both the discovery of and witness for personal and corporate spiritual renewal. The hesitancy that some feel about what is emerging is due to the feeling that the search for God's revelation will be diluted to humanitarian deeds only. If this happens, then the dynamic of faith will find no more satisfactory results than those achieved during the past fifteen years.

The "crisis of faith" at the beginning of the 1970s has come to be expressed in terms of the techniques of evangelism as much as in terms of the theology of evangelism. The theology of evangelism for the 1970s requires more than personal repentance, confession of faith, and commitment—important as these are.

Prior to the 1970s evangelism was frequently looked upon as a kind of personal salvation. Man's response was essentially his own doing and there was little recognition of God's working in the life of the individual. Church membership meant a kind of social acceptability. People became members of the church because it was the thing to do.

Looking back upon those years, we see clearly that millions "joined" the church as an institution in society but never fully committed themselves to respond to God's mission revealed in Jesus Christ in the world. The result was circumscribed either by the change in the individual's personal life or by his support of mission projects designed to bring enlightenment to the heathen far away. Nevertheless, there was bright evidence of those who responded to God's mission: the development and work of the Salvation Army, the woman's suffrage movement, Hull House, Church World Service, and community service. These and others gave expression of the Christian gospel through social reform.

The theology of the 1970s is a clear call for man to understand that God is working in each individual and in the whole world. The individual is required by the kind of world in which he lives and the call of God to love his fellowman and to express that love by individual and corporate service to his fellowman. The central task of evangelism, therefore, is to confront every individual with the calling of God revealed in Christ in the world and to seek the commitment of each individual to respond to that call.

Paul put it this way: " ... work out your own salvation with fear and trembling; for God is at work in you, both to will and to work for his good pleasure" (Phil. 2:12–13). In this statement, Paul leads us to believe that conversion is not a simple once-for-all event in life. Though he makes it clear elsewhere that God through Jesus Christ has redeemed man, the fact remains that man must respond to what God has done and must continue to respond to what God continues to do. Though the primary task of evangelism is to confront man with the Good News and to elicit his beginning response, it remains the task of the whole fellowship of the congregation to sustain, support, encourage, and seek to enable the individual in "working out his own salvation" in day-to-day response to God at work in him and in the world.

Techniques of Evangelism

The techniques of evangelism have always been many and diverse. Within the past twenty years, the following have been predominant among many Protestant denominations:

- Mass evangelism
- Visitation evangelism (sometimes called two-by-two evangelism)
- Fireside evangelism
- Youth evangelism

The object of all four techniques was and is securing commitment of the individual to the cause of Christ. They are best understood in relation to the method of communication involved in each.

Mass evangelism seeks to communicate the Good News of God through preaching the gospel, singing hymns, and arousing emotion in great mass meetings, frequently called revivals. Mass evangelism is possibly the best known of all evangelistic methods because it is that which seemed to be practiced at Pentecost (Acts 2). It was used by John Wesley, Cotton Mather, Jonathan Edwards, Charles Reign Scoville, Billy Sunday, and early evangelists of the Christian Church (Disciples of Christ) such as Barton W. Stone and Walter Scott. Billy Graham is currently the strongest exponent of mass evangelism. Mass evangelism seeks the conversion of the individual, produces a personal piety, and normally does not direct its efforts toward changing the social systems of man. Whatever may be said against mass evangelism, it must be recognized that many of the people who today claim Christ as Lord and are seeking real change in the world are the product of mass evangelism.

Visitation evangelism became popular in the 1950s and 1960s but had diminishing effect in the last half of the decade of the sixties. The object of visitation evangelism is not different from that of mass evangelism. As a matter of fact, visitation evangelism seeks the commitment of the individual to the church. But it does not deal in any real measure with the social responsibilities of the individual in response to the mission of God as revealed in the world. Visitation evangelism, however, seeks to personalize evangelism by sending people out two-by-two into the community, city, or countryside to confront individuals and families with the Good News of the Master.

Fireside evangelism does not differ in objective from mass and visitation evangelism. Neither does it differ in its view of social action. Its difference rests in method. An individual or a family seeks to reach other individuals or families through small meetings in homes. Here a conversational type of confrontation takes place and some study begins to open the way for new understanding of the social implications of the Good News.

Youth evangelism is sometimes associated with or serves as a part of mass, visitation, or fireside evangelism. One evidence of this kind of evangelism is the youth crusades that have sprung up during the past decade. They are primarily an extension of mass evangelism incorporated within a movement of youth. The major fault in the crusades on college campuses and elsewhere is that they do not necessarily move people to respond to what God is doing in the world but seek only the commitment of the individual to Christ as Lord and Savior.

New Dimensions

Sociology, sensitivity awareness, and new understandings of the arts of communication have brought changes to evangelism and will likely be the most important factors shaping evangelism in the years to come.

In the 1960s, sociology gave man a new awareness of himself—an awareness that would turn him outward to his fellowman, not in upon himself. Man began the task of discovering whose, who, and what he was. The result has been the renewal of the church through those persons who have dared to see themselves as "sons of man" designed to respond to God's call through Christ and to serve man in the world.

Sensitivity awareness, a product of behavioristic sociology and psychology, has helped to release man from himself and to turn him toward others. This has come about in his discovery of whose, who, and what he is and by his willingness to communicate with others in an open and free manner. It is the learning to hear and be heard, to listen and be listened to, to speak and be spoken to. It is the thrill of understanding more than words, even comprehending the movement of the hands, head, and body as a part of the art of communication. *Understanding Media* by Marshall H. McLuhan opened the thought of man in the 1960s to the understanding that the media of communication are an extension of man's mind, voice, and act of communicating.

Evangelism has begun to grasp new ways to serve. The result has been the development of what is being called and increasingly recognized as face-to-face evangelism.

Face-to-face evangelism is the eye-to-eye confrontation of the individual with the best understanding of sensitivity awareness and the best possible use of the arts of communication in order to bring him to respond to God's call through Christ in the world. It is designed to give the individual the opportunity to become a vital part of a congregation—the koinonia—and to respond to God's love by loving and serving others. It is no longer enough to do many things of the past. It is not enough for man to begin the long pilgrimage of responding to what God is doing in the world. This means being confronted by the Good News and, recognizing that God is working through each of us, to accept him as revealed through Christ as Lord and Savior. This is a conversion of the individual which must find fulfillment in the conversion of the persons, society, and systems surrounding each individual.

The objective of evangelism has changed as have its theology and methods. The objective is to bring man and his abilities to God's mission and to become a participating servant in that mission of reconciliation in the whole world.

Each congregation should use the evangelism technique that best fulfills its desired response to God's mission. It is possible to use the tried methods of evangelism, providing they are directed to the development of the individual and congregational action of Christian witness, which is beyond personal salvation.

Organization in Brief

The work of evangelism in the congregation may be developed through a committee, department, commission, or task group, responsible to the general board of the congregation. Plans are coordinated into the total program of the congregation through the church cabinet.

An evangelism committee, department, commission, or task group may consist of three or more members. However, it may secure additional workers. One congregation in Missouri carries on a year-round program of evangelism conducted by a committee of twelve. The committee meets monthly to plan its work and, because it has a program of visitation evangelism, to make calls.

An evangelism committee, department, commission, or task group may be composed of those who plan and carry out the work of evangelism in the congregation; or it may be brought into existence by the general board once or twice a year to conduct special evangelistic emphases, such as youth evangelism, visitation evangelism, face-to-face evangelism, etc.

The minister is essential to the success of the congregation's evangelism work with respect to both planning and carrying out the plans. It is his administrative guidance and spiritual motivation that will spell much of the success or failure of the congregation's attitude and work in the area of evangelism.

10

Mission Action Through Education

Christian education has the task of "drawing out" the individual to the fullest possible realization of his potential. Education provides the opportunity for the individual to learn facts in various arenas of life and sets him about the task of expressing in action the meaning of what he has learned.

Christian education is described in the following manner by the Department of Christian Education of the Division of Homeland Ministries of the Christian Church (Disciples of Christ):

Education in the ministry of the Christian community is the activity or service of teaching-learning.... Its particular work is:

- to introduce persons to the heritage, fellowship, mission and ministry of the Christian community.
- to lead persons into or confirm them in an intentional relationship within the community based upon decision and commitment to discipleship in response to the person and call of Jesus Christ.
- to nurture persons in a growing understanding of their own identity as Christians, of the nature and life of the community, and of the world God is bringing to be.
- to guide their individual becoming or growth, and their grow-

ing and deepening involvement in the life, mission and ministry of the community and in the world.

Teaching-learning experiences may be planned or unplanned. The planned experiences in the congregation include special study classes, retreats, camps, conferences, church school classes, through-the-week education, classes for the mentally retarded; study groups of Christian Women's Fellowship, Christian Men's Fellowship, and youth groups; special home study and opportunities provided for training leaders in all aspects of the congregation's program.

The program and materials for planned teaching-learning experiences are called curriculum. The Christian Church (Disciples of Christ) has made a great investment of time, work, and financial resources to develop the Christian Life Curriculum. For the church's school there are two series of materials: Perspective Series and Uniform Series. Both are built upon the same objective:

> . . . that all persons respond to God in faith and love—being aware of his self-disclosure and especially of his redeeming love as revealed in Jesus Christ—so that they may come to know who they are and what their human situation means, grow as sons of God rooted in the Christian community, live in the Spirit of God in every relationship, fulfill their common discipleship in the world, and abide in the Christian hope.[1]

The Perspective Series and the Uniform Series of the Christian Life Curriculum are shaped around the "crossing point" proposition: "that man's persistent life needs are intersected by the will of God revealed in Jesus Christ." From this confrontation emerges new life meanings for each individual. This is an exciting venture in the teaching-learning experience and provides the congregation with the op-

1. Richard E. Lentz, Paul H. Vieth, and Ray L. Henthorne, *Our Teaching Ministry* (St. Louis: Christian Board of Publication, 1967), pp. 135–36.

portunity to develop new life qualities and understandings among its members.

Teaching-learning experiences may be unplanned. Such experiences may take place within the regular and planned educational opportunities provided by the congregation, but they are not limited to what happens in these specific situations. On the contrary, the congregation is engaged in teaching-learning experiences in all of its life and wherever the individuals may find themselves.

Unplanned teaching-learning experiences may take place on a planned field trip of a regular church school class. For example, a child suffers a minor accident and bruises a knee. The showing of Christian love, compassion, and concern in such a situation provides the opportunity for an unplanned teaching-learning experience. Such opportunities also occur in the home, community, school, and business life of people both within and outside the congregation. The sharing of joy, sadness, and unexpected tragedy all become unplanned teaching-learning experiences.

Providing teaching-learning experiences that meet the needs of the people should have high priority for the entire congregation. This will require considerable flexibility in the courses to be studied and the materials to be used. The Christian Life Curriculum provides for this kind of flexibility in the settings on Christian Living Encounters and retreats. The unscheduled areas in both settings provide opportunities for congregations to carry out their own courses as needed. The church's school series of courses, however, is designed to provide basic training and should be followed carefully. Nevertheless, flexibility in the area of teaching-learning experiences for adults, young people, and children should be used where needed. Such experiences should be closely related to the people's need for community studies and action, intensive study in theology, etc.

The church's ministry in teaching-learning experiences might well observe what is happening in public education in the United States. "In April, 1969, the Danforth and Ford Foundations sponsored a conference in Washington, D. C., on 'The School and the Democratic Environment.' The purpose of the conference was to explore how the schools can better prepare young people to function in a democratic society beset by unprecedented demands and complexity."[2] Robert H. Finch, former secretary of the Department of Health, Education and Welfare of the federal government, had this to say: "Freedom is not something spoonfed in a civics class. It is a state of being, and it must be experienced as a matter of daily affirmation."[3]

Young people of high school age are known to say, "Freedom is something we are taught about in the classroom and something we can experience only in the streets." Reading this kind of statement raises the question, How different are the teaching-learning experiences of the congregation? Ramsey Clark, former United States Attorney General, points out, "... we must remember that while some crave order and others seek justice, the long history of man says, in school or in life, you will have neither order nor justice unless you have both."[4]

The whole matter of Christian education is as much under attack as is the public education system. It is likely that most people are no longer willing to spend their time learning more and more facts. They want to see how those facts can be translated into action.

To repeat the opening sentence of this chapter, Christian education has the task of "drawing out" the individual to the fullest possible realization of his potential. Two years

2. *The School and the Democratic Environment* (New York: Columbia University Press, 1970), p. v.

3. Ibid., p. 25.

4. Ibid., p. 37.

ago three women became intrigued with a Christian Women's Fellowship study session dealing with women volunteering their services in community projects. They decided to see what they could do in this field. They began as volunteer counselors in a prison in the area. As of this writing, twenty families of their congregation are engaged in this service as well as serving as tutors and helpers in the public school system and serving as volunteers in a housing project in the neighborhood. There is more to do than they can accomplish. One woman said of her work, "God gave me my life, and I am having the best time of my life in the work of volunteer service." This is what can happen when the teaching-learning experience is really the "drawing out" of the individual in response to what God is doing in the world.

Not everybody can or will make this kind of response, but to have a lesser objective of the teaching-learning experiences in the congregation is to deny the working of God in life and to miss the joys of the life of Christian service.

Organization in Brief

Each congregation will find it helpful to have a committee, department, commission, or task group working on education in the life of the congregation, responsible to the general board of the congregation, its work coordinated into the total work of the congregation through the cabinet. The minister is the master teacher in the context of the curriculum. He does not teach all courses, but he may find it helpful to teach the key courses designed to be used each year with the leaders of the congregation's educational ministry. In addition, the minister is the one person responsible for the overall development of the congregation's educational ministry.

The committee, department, commission, or task group on education should be composed of those persons responsible for each of the settings in the Christian Life Curriculum, including leadership development. Meetings of this group should be held quarterly and, in some instances, more frequently if needed.

11

Mission Action Through Worship

Worship is the expression of thanksgiving and joy both to and for God revealed through Jesus Christ in the world. It is the recognition by man that God is worthy of praise, thanksgiving, and joy. Worship provides the opportunity for spiritual renewal of persons and congregations in responding to God's mission.

The theology of worship has all too frequently been built upon a concept of God as being "out there." Man's worship in such a context was always directed to a God who had to be moved to doing what was good for man—or what man thought was good for his well-being—through sacrifice, penitence, and prayer. Such acts of worship fell into certain accepted forms which man historically assumed would achieve his ends. In modern times, such worship is often expressed in services—planned for a specific time—of praise, prayer, hymns, reading of scripture, exhortation, and benediction. It has been assumed, somehow, that the individual's fulfillment of this ritual—even as seldom as once a week—is a sufficient response to God. In certain cultures the success of the individual in business, community, and home life was sufficient evidence that he was on the right course.

Another approach to the meaning of man's praise, thanksgiving, and worship is that out of such experiences the individual will be motivated to new meanings in life. Obviously the power of the Holy Spirit to work in the life of man through acts of worship has long been accepted by Christian communities. Worship may provide the climate in which God works his will in the hearts of men, but it is not a means of guaranteeing that God will do what man desires.

The new theology of worship brings freshness to the acts of worship as celebration of what God is doing and what man does in response to God's mission. The result is worshiping when there is reason to worship and not just because the hour of worship has arrived. Man worships regularly as a discipline for preparation for God's leading and as a celebration of praise, thanksgiving, and joy for what God has effected in his life.

Worship may be individual and corporate. In both instances it may be guided or spontaneous. Guided worship provides the discipline for the individual to be open to the movement of God's will. Spontaneous worship is that kind of ecstatic expression made necessary because of the abounding joy and gratitude or the sudden calamity, sadness, or guilt in the life of the worshiper. Such worship may be the result of the individual's response to God's working in the world and at other times the breaking forth of the joy in the heart of an individual for God's goodness to him. Both kinds of worship, guided and spontaneous, are true celebrations.

Individual worship of a guided or disciplined nature requires the worshiper to provide some time each day, or some regular times each week, when he can read from the Scriptures or great literature of men of the spirit, meditate on these words, and seek understanding of himself and new meanings for life. This kind of individual worship is not to be confused with regular corporate worship, which, although important, provides a different kind of opportunity for the worshiper.

Corporate worship provides the opportunity for the individual and the group to support each other in one of the meaningful expressions of the congregation as koinonia. Sharing in the acts of praise, singing hymns, reading scripture, participating in the Lord's Supper, and exhortation allow mutual expression of support to each other and praise to God. Spiritual renewal of the individual may come in corporate worship just as in individual worship. Motivation for future action in mission and the opportunity to celebrate God's mighty acts in the world and life of man are present in both individual and corporate worship.

Worship in the corporate sense may take many and varied forms. In past years it centered around the pulpit. However, in a sense the pulpit is isolated. The minister speaks, the congregation listens, but there is no helpful dialogue. Increasingly, within the past decade, ministers in various congregations have instituted coffee hours or talk-back sessions immediately following the worship service where the laity can discuss the sermon with the minister.

Some ministers, as a result of study in sensitivity training, have developed a kind of roving style of preaching that takes them out of the pulpit into the congregation where questions may be introduced and discussed as a part of the sermon. Such a practice requires a minister who is mature and free from inhibitions concerning his self-understanding. Of course, there is a certain risk in such a procedure, but the openness offered by it is a healthy part of the preaching-prophetic ministry. Such a practice will, among other things, ensure that the minister knows what the needs and thoughts of the people are, to the end that his labors may be more relevant to those needs.

Other forms of worship are indicated by a move from the formal setting of the chancel, nave, and pews. Many congregations throughout the country are turning—partly because of the high cost of building—to the development of space for multiple use. The space used for worship is also frequently used for fellowship, recreation, and teaching-learning experiences. One of the oldest congregations in the Midwest, Christ Church Cathedral (Episcopal), in St. Louis, Missouri, has a newly designed altar with the congregational seating arranged in a rectangle around the four sides of the altar. This has provided the congregation with a new sense of togetherness and opportunities for more meaningful worship experiences. Churches in the round are to be found in many places across the country. Out-of-door worship has been common at camps and conferences and is becoming more frequently used by congregations.

New forms of worship include new styles of music, use of instruments other than the piano and organ, and use of liturgical colors and liturgical orders of worship.

New forms of worship and new styles of church buildings indicate that man is seeking to worship God as he is moved to worship. Ritual is changing. Man is beginning to break into a new freedom that allows him the privilege of using both the religious and secular to express praise, thanksgiving, and joy to God.

Perhaps in worship the church is faced with one of the greatest dilemmas of its modern life. Each congregation is composed of basically two congregations—one young and the other middle-aged and elderly. The generation gap is most evident in the congregation at the point of worship. Some people in the middle-aged and elderly group want to hold to the older patterns of worship; the youth—no less committed to worship—want to find new expressions of their praise, thanksgiving, and joy for what God is doing in the world and what he means to their lives. Some congregations meet this dilemma by holding two worship services—one directed toward the youth and using experimental styles of worship, and the other directed toward the other members of the congregation, using more traditional forms of worship. Some congregations vary their worship services every two or three Sundays. This provides some tensions but has the virtue of providing the opportunity for understanding on the part of all in the congregation.

Worship is at the heart of the life of the congregation. It can motivate to higher forms of service and provide opportunity for the individual and the congregation to celebrate experiences of service that are meaningful for both the individual and the congregation. Worship can provide the opportunity for the individual and congregation to discover a true oneness with God in life equal to that of the servanthood acts. It is because of this that worship is given as a characteristic of the congregation as church in mission. The minister is the enabler of worship in the highest and best sense in each congregation.

Organization in Brief

The worship committee, department, commission, or task group is responsible to the general board of the congregation, with its plans coordinated into the whole life of the congregation by the church cabinet. The size of the group should be adequate for the needs of the congregation. It should represent—as should all committees, departments, commissions, and task groups—men and women, youth and older people, and peoples of all races. This will make evident the contribution of many different individuals and cultures to worship.

The worship group should plan for the development of the individual and corporate spiritual life of the congregation and the surrounding community. This includes experimentation in new forms and styles of worship and providing the essential equipment for worship, such as hymnals, worship bulletins, musical instruments, and other physical equipment. The worship group should be responsible for the choral groups of the congregation, including the administration of the leadership of such groups.

12

Mission Action Through Stewardship

Stewardship may seem to be a word of clouded theological meaning; for some the word is no longer meaningful. One congregation has sought to exchange the word *stewardship* for *money*. Stewardship deals with the responsible use of money, but it involves more than money. To limit stewardship to money is to miss much of the real richness and depth of its meaning.

Stewardship is the responsible use of all of life, including money, by both individual and congregation in response to God's mission as revealed through Christ in the world. It may be asked, "What is meant by the responsible use of life? Stewardship begins with the whole of life, that is, the whole of the individual's resources as well as the whole of the congregation's resources. This includes the fact of being alive, the talents, time, and money at the disposal of the individual or the group.

Responsible use of all life requires that the individual and the congregation begin with an examination of how much of their resources (time, talent, and money) is being used in response to God's mission.

The psalmist indicated the purpose of life with these words:

> I give thanks to thee, O Lord my God, with my whole heart,
> and I will glorify thy name for ever.
>
> —Psalm 86:12

Christ, in the early part of the Sermon on the Mount, put it this way: "You are the light of the world.... Let your light so shine before men, that they may see your good works and give glory to your Father who is in heaven" (Matt. 5: 14, 16).

The purpose of the individual Christian—and this is no less true of the corporate life of the congregation—is to glorify God with all of life. Consequently, stewardship is not to be understood as what is "set aside for God and his work" but is to be understood in terms of how all of life and its resources are used day by day.

Stewardship requires a constancy throughout all of life. For example, the constancy of life is shattered by the individual or group that supports programs and work to feed the hungry, shelter the homeless, and clothe the naked at the same time it supports those social systems that charge exorbitant prices for food sold to the poor, manage and perpetuate substandard housing in the ghetto, or seek to give cast-off, shabby clothing to the poor. Stewardship that glorifies God must be consistent; it should be evident in the systems of society as well as in personal sharing.

Responsible stewardship requires that the individual whenever possible meet his own human needs, but not at the expense of another. Starvation is still starvation whether it is experienced by the poor who do not have enough to eat or by the affluent who suffer malnutrition. Both kinds are the result of inadequate stewardship, and both deny the opportunity for the individual to respond to God's mission. The adequate meeting of human need for all is essential to any meaningful understanding of stewardship.

Stewardship requires the setting aside of a portion of life's resources (time, talents, and money) for use by others to meet human need. When the individual or group decides how large the portion should be, stewardship becomes deeply meaningful. For example, an individual, family, or group may decide to spend 97 percent of its resources for meeting its own needs and to give 3 percent to the church and/or community for meeting the needs of others. Each year this decision should be made anew because the individual, family, or group situation may change, allowing for an increase in the life resources to be used for others.

Stewardship requires the setting of great objectives in the use of resources by the individual, family, or group. Such an objective may be the giving of a portion of 10 percent or more. Some may achieve this goal within a single year, while others may find it possible to achieve such a goal within two or three years. However, such achievement will be based upon continual study by the individual, family, or group of what God's mission is and what human needs are visible, plus an abiding awareness that God has an increasing dominion over the life of the individual, family, or group.

Stewardship requires the meeting of human need. This may be done by verbal proclamation of the Good News of Jesus Christ; teaching the illiterate to read; providing aid to the hungry, sick, or dying; finding jobs for the unemployed; registering individuals to vote; or a thousand other things that make evident man's achievement in his struggle for human dignity and the expression of love to all mankind.

Meeting human need may be accomplished through the church at the congregational, regional, or general level. It may be accomplished through community enterprises. It may be accomplished within the United States and Canada or in overseas ministries of the church or secular organizations. Obviously, the church is very effective in meeting human need. However, it can no longer be assumed that the church is the only organization capable of this.

Stewardship provides the means whereby action in mission can be engaged beyond the reach of the individual, family, or group. Obviously each individual or group cannot go everywhere and do everything. It is possible, however, through that portion set aside, for every individual and group to make effective response to God's mission through service to others. It is this fulfillment of God's mission that glorifies not only God but also the life of the individual. As Jesus approached the time of his crucifixion and his betrayer was identified, it is recorded that Jesus said, "Now is the Son of man glorified, and in him God is glorified; ..." (John 13: 31). Stewardship makes possible the kind of mission action that brings meaning to the life of the individual, family, or group and thereby glorifies both it and God.

Stewardship is mission in action. Without sound stewardship and financial support the witness of the congregation—both individual and corporate—will be unable to move. A sound program is necessary; without it the congregation will not respond. However, without financial support the best program will be useless.

Organization in Brief

A stewardship committee, department, commission, or task group should be responsible for oversight of the stewardship concerns of the congregation, including stewardship education. The group should work cooperatively with the worship group of the congregation and the minister so that effective worship resources will be used and theological positions supportive of Christian stewardship will be presented.

The stewardship committee, department, commission, or

task group may serve as the finance committee of the congregation. In some instances the finance function may be provided by a subcommittee of the stewardship group. In still other situations, the finance committee may be a separate group within the life of the congregation.

The finance group is to promote and provide information regarding the congregation's financial needs, including its expression of mission action both at home and overseas. This group is not responsible for setting forth the financial needs in a budget that it believes acceptable to the congregation, but it is responsible for keeping the congregation informed about those needs as it seeks to respond to God's mission in the world. This stance requires that the finance group essentially derive its information about financial needs from the whole life of the congregation and through the other committees, departments, commissions, and task groups.

The congregation should, by its vote and the commitment of its resources, determine the response it wishes to make to God's mission. For a committee—even the finance committee—to take this prerogative from the members of the congregation is to deny them the responsibility of effective action based upon sound information and the guidance of the Holy Spirit.

The finance group, through the work of the financial secretary and the treasurer of the congregation, is responsible for the records of both the income and the expenditures of the congregation. The budget, which reflects the congregation's response to God's mission, should be approved by majority vote of the general board of the congregation and by a majority vote of the congregation. Dispersal of funds by the treasurer that differs from what is allowed in the budget should be approved by both the general board and the congregation. Although this principle should be followed in all matters related to expenditures, it is especially true when a solution to a local financial crisis is sought by use of funds from the outreach budget. This is not only financially unsound; it is morally and spiritually unsound. Congregation after congregation has proved that the fellowship which keeps faith with its outreach commitments will find the way to meet its other needs. The root issue at this point is not so much one of dollars and cents as it is one of spiritual commitment.

The work of the stewardship and finance group(s) should be coordinated through the work of the cabinet and responsible to the general board. The final authority of the congregation is essential in finalizing its financial needs and expenditures each year.

There are diverse procedures that the stewardship and finance group(s) may use in securing the support of individuals and groups for the financial needs of the congregation. Each congregation should adopt the procedure that seems most helpful to its style of life and witness. Some common concerns should face each congregation in establishing its financial needs and in securing the financial support to meet these needs. Some of these are as follows:

- Every member of the congregation should have adequate opportunity to assume his responsibility for determining the budget.

- There should be adequate salary for competent leadership.

- Property and grounds should be adequately maintained.

- All properties should have sufficient insurance coverage.

- Adequate pension or social security funding, or both, and accident insurance should be provided.

- There should be adequate materials and equipment for

the care and growth of the individual and corporate life of the congregation.

- The goal of 50-50 giving should be set; that is, the congregation should try to give as much to others as it keeps for itself.
- Every member of the congregation and every other person involved in its life and work should be given the opportunity to help support the congregation's financial needs.
- An Every Member Commitment Program should be conducted in the congregation annually or no less often than biennially.

The Every Member Commitment Program is of great importance and deserves careful planning and the ablest of leadership. The program may be conducted annually or biennially. Various forms of the program may provide increased effectiveness. When the task is approached as an act and opportunity of spiritual importance, the rewards to the life of the congregation far exceed monetary measurements; and generally the funds will be provided for the congregation's response to God's mission (see Appendix A).

13

Mission Action Through Social Involvement

Social action is one kind of action toward which evangelism, education, worship, and stewardship are pointed. It has its roots in the Scriptures:

> "Woe to those who lie upon beds of ivory,
> and stretch themselves upon their couches,
> and eat lambs from the flock,
> and calves from the midst of the stall;
> who sing idle songs to the sound of the harp,
> and like David invent for themselves
> instruments of music;
> who drink wine in bowls,
> and anoint themselves with the finest oils,
> but are not grieved over the ruin of Joseph!"
> —Amos 6:4–6

> "He has showed you, O man, what is good;
> and what does the LORD require of you
> but to do justice, and to love kindness,
> and to walk humbly with your God?"
> —Micah 6:8

"Then the King will say to those at his right hand, 'Come, O blessed of my Father, inherit the kingdom prepared for you from the foundation of the world; for I was hungry and you gave me food, I was thirsty and you gave me drink, I was a stranger and you welcomed me, I was naked and you clothed me, I was sick and you visited me, I was in prison and you came to me" (Matt. 25:34–36).

"Now in these days when the disciples were increasing in number, the Hellenists murmured against the Hebrews because their widows were neglected in the daily distribution. And the twelve summoned the body of the disciples and said, 'It is not right that we should give up preaching the word of God to serve tables. Therefore, brethren, pick out from among you seven men of good repute, full of the Spirit and of wisdom, whom we may appoint to this duty'" (Acts 6:1–3).

Social involvement is the practical and applied expression of response to God's mission in day-to-day conduct of life. It is the fulfilling of theology in terms of ethical conduct between individuals and groups.

The history of social involvement begins with God's concern expressed in the creation story when he said: "... and you shall eat the plants of the field. In the sweat of your face you shall eat bread ..." (Gen. 3:18–19). God assured man of the plenitude of food upon the earth. The ancient Hebrew was taught, as his descendants are taught in the synagogue today, to share food with the wayfarer and stranger.

Concern for ethical conduct is in evidence along the course of man's history. Francis of Assisi (1182–1226) founded the order of Franciscans and taught reverence for life and service to those in need. Loyola (1491–1556), the founder of the Society of Jesus, also bore witness to his concern for those in need.

It was William Booth (1829–1912) who, in East London, responded to the call of the poor and organized the Salvation Army. Charles Dickens, writing about the tragedy of human need that was part of the industrial revolution, brought a rising tide of response from those who acted as a part of God's mission in the world.

The swelling tide of those who expressed their concern for human need and sought to serve the poor included Jane Addams of Hull House, Chicago, Illinois; poets such as Edwin Markham; and novelists such as Mark Twain. Henry Nelson Wieman and Walter Marshall Horton, in 1938, wrote these words:

> This practical, ethical form of modern theology has had a great influence in America, where it chimes in with the pragmatist movement in philosophy, and the general American tendency to stress useful ethical activity at the expense of deep feeling or precise thought. It goes very commonly with a strong emphasis upon the need of a social application of Christian principles—as in the teaching of Walter Rauschenbusch.[1]

It was, perhaps, the teaching of Walter Rauschenbusch that awakened the social gospel movement in America at the beginning of the twentieth century. Social concern today is the product of two world wars and the Korean and Vietnam wars, together with the Great Depression of the 1930s. From the theology of neoorthodoxy of the 1920s to the early 1960s there has come a new theology of existentialism. The roots of existentialism are in Kierkegaard and later German philosophers and theologians. One value of existentialism is that it has awakened a new concern for the individual person in particular and man and his human condition in general.

1. *The Growth of Religion* (New York: Willett, Clark & Company, 1938), pp. 186–87.

Social involvement at the beginning of the 1970s has taken on a vitality only dreamed of by Rauschenbusch and his predecessors. The social application of the Good News of Christ as a response to what God is doing in the world has caught the imagination and dedication of youth especially and of an increasing number of other people in the United States and other nations. The emergence of black, brown, and red power groups stimulated by the leadership of Martin Luther King, Jr., and others is bringing into sharper focus the issues of man's human situation. Issues such as peace, nuclear weapons, hunger, the population explosion, justice, and the pollution of air, soil, and water have turned man to a new kind of action.

Demonstrations, both peaceful and not-so-peaceful, involvement in politics, participation in the world of business and finance, and a vital attempt to change the systems in society are only part of the new kind of social action. The Good News of Christ is no longer a personal matter only. It calls for change in the life of the individual and the use of the individual's life in changing the society in which he lives. Christianity is no longer viable as a one-day-a-week religion; it is viable only as the full-time work of all who have given their lives in response to God's mission in the world.

Social involvement has become a style of life for many people who earnestly seek to follow in the way of the Master. It is no longer enough to give money to be spent by others in feeding the poor and clothing the naked. The earnest Christian will give his money and, in addition, he will give his time and talents to help provide better housing, better jobs, better education, and better life in general for the poor spread across the world. These words from the Bible are a judgment on society: "If any one says, 'I love God,' and hates his brother, he is a liar; for he who does not love his brother whom he has seen, cannot love God whom he has not seen" (1 John 4:20).

Social involvement, like evangelism, education, worship, and stewardship, is essential to the life of the congregation. It is less than easy to develop the social expression of the Good News in some congregations. There are those who say, "The church has no business in politics, business, schools, etc." It is difficult to understand this argument. The Master spoke sharply about the practices of the church and of the government under which he lived. His voice was raised for the people of the land and he was championed mostly by the common and poor people of his day. He sought to be loyal to both his church and his government, but he also sought to reform life in his day. For that—and precisely for that—he was put to death.

Difficult as the task may be, the Christian must respond to God's mission in the world—*the whole world*—through all of his life. The same is required of the entire congregation.

It should be noted that pursuing this task will put the Christian under some tension, if not conflict, both as an individual and as part of the corporate life of the congregation. Dealing with such conflict requires skill, love, and a high sense of integrity. For specific suggestions in dealing with conflict, see chapter 8.

Organization in Brief

The congregation's social involvement program may be developed through the work of a committee, department, commission, or task group. In some congregations, the committee, department, or commission is basically a task group or a collection of task groups engaged in specific tasks throughout each year. Such should be organized under the authority of the general board of the congregation and coordinated through the work of the cabinet. If the congregation does not provide for such action in its organized life, then individuals interested in the work of social involvement may form an ad hoc group for this purpose. This group should have communication with the minister and the general board.

The social involvement program of the congregation will be confronted with emergency needs such as helping a family meet a crisis resulting from loss of employment, illness, or accident; working for peace by supporting or not supporting specific legislation at the federal government level; supporting or not supporting welfare legislation at the city, state, or federal government level. These emergencies call for quick response on the part of responsible individuals and groups. For example, it is difficult to predict when the United States Senate or House of Representatives will vote on an issue. Consequently, letters, phone calls, and telegrams are needed at a moment's notice. The social involvement group must be prepared to respond quickly and effectively.

All people in the congregation—men, women, and youth—have a part to play in social involvement. Following are a few suggestions of what can be undertaken by a committee, department, commission, or task group:

- Support the search for peace.
- Support the struggle for improved race relations.
- Support the preservation of natural resources.
- Engage in interracial activities.
- Support better housing for the poor.
- Support improved education in the community, especially for the poor.
- Support programs of literacy and on-the-job training that aid the poor.

- Support the work to find improved employment for all, especially the poor.
- Support adequate health services to the community, especially those in the community who are poor.
- Support volunteer programs of service to public schools, hospitals, rest homes, prisons, and housing projects.
- Support candidates and legislative and political activities that are pledged to remedy the needs indicated above.

Support of this kind of work requires more than financial giving. It requires the heart and hands of people.

Social involvement provides the means of change in the lives of members of the congregation and in the life of the community. It is time-consuming work, but it is the kind of work that gives each person engaged in it the joy of discovering how faith is translated into deeds.

14

Mission Action Through Outreach

Outreach is essential to the congregation's fulfillment of its response to God's mission. It includes support through study, money, and personal involvement in Christian ministry and witness beyond the congregation and its immediate community. Outreach is specifically responsible for the congregation's knowledge and support of, and involvement in, the following areas of work in the Christian Church (Disciples of Christ):

ministry and witness

- of the general manifestation of the church (national and international)
- of the regional manifestation of the church (state/area)
- overseas
- at home (in the United States and Canada)
- in higher education (undergraduate and seminary)
- to the homeless, orphaned, and aged
- in ministerial relief

While the congregation supports the varied work of the

church in differing degrees, outreach is specifically responsible for providing the congregation with information and securing support of the work of the church beyond the congregation and its immediate community. The financial support of the work of the church is remitted through the regular promotional office of the church.

For the purposes of this book, the following areas of ministry and witness will be considered: overseas, at home, in higher education, and to the homeless, orphaned, and aged.

One of the dangers in the current awakening to human need at home is that the congregation may be turned inward in a new way. That is, the congregation, in turning outward to the community at home, may turn inward or away from the larger community of the world. What is needed is a sense of balance and proportion that allows the congregation the opportunity to respond to the full dimension of God's mission in the whole world. This means that the congregation is required to respond to the needs of the fellowship (koinonia), the community at home, and the world overseas.

Outreach Overseas

The outreach overseas thrust of the Good News is as old as the church itself. The ancient Hebrews sought to take their faith to the world beyond their own tribes. In New Testament times, Paul was the chief leader in the spread of Christianity to a major part of the Roman world. The following New Testament references are basic to the overseas ministry thrust of the Good News:

> "For God so loved the world that he gave his only Son, that whoever believes in him should not perish but have eternal life" (John 3:16).
>
> "You are the salt of the earth ..." (Matt. 5:13).
>
> "You are the light of the world" (Matt. 5:14).

"He who sows the good seed is the Son of man; the field is the world ..." (Matt. 13:37–38).

"The true light that enlightens every man was coming into the world. He was in the world, and the world was made through him, yet the world knew him not.... And the Word became flesh and dwelt among us, full of grace and truth; we have beheld his glory, glory as of the only Son from the Father" (John 1: 9–10, 14).

"Go therefore and make disciples of all nations ..." (Matt. 28:19). Jesus and his followers had a cosmic view of the Good News, and the early church caught this vision. The fire of this passion has not dimmed through the years. The development of the monastic movement, the university movement of the Renaissance, and the great revivals all testify to the vitality of this cosmic vision.

The development of outreach overseas was early evidenced in the Roman Catholic Church with its sending of missionaries to the Goths, England, and Ireland. Prior to the birth of the missionary movement on the shores of the New World, the work of the evangelicals and the Methodists in England had brought about the establishment of the work of foreign missions in England with offices in London. Overseas ministry took on a special power and organization as early as the beginning of the nineteenth century in the United States.

In the summer of 1806 a little group of students at Williams College, Massachusetts, taking a walk across the fields and discussing as they walked, were caught by a thunderstorm and took refuge under a haystack. There, storm and all, their conversation went on. One of their number had expressed tremendous concern about the unfulfilled command of our Lord, "Go ye." He felt that nothing was being done by the Church in the United States about taking the gospel to the far corners of the earth.

As he and his friends talked, they became convinced that the Lord was calling them to that task, and that they must stir the Church to action. They knelt beneath the haystack for prayer—long and earnest prayer—and they rose with a slogan, "We can, if we will. We must, if we can." The movement in the United States for foreign missions started from these college students. One of their number, seeing that someone must go up and down the land to awaken the Church to the idea, gave up his personal ambition to be one of the pioneers overseas, to be instead the "promoter." Several of the others went overseas as the first missionaries. And from them the momentum rolled to fulfillment in spectacular fashion.[1]

The movement that began interdenominationally soon became a denominational program. Adoniram Judson was sent to Burma, and literally thousands have gone to the whole world from all the denominations in the past one hundred and sixty years. It is something of a paradox that the movement in the United States, which began as interdenominational and then became denominational in character, is at last becoming ecumenical. Through the World Missionary Organization, which has become a part of the World Council of Churches, the work of overseas ministry is being increasingly conducted with closer ecumenical support and is beginning to develop a unified witness in response to God's mission in the world.

The Christian Church (Disciples of Christ) began its own involvement in overseas outreach with the organization of the American Missionary Society in 1849 (see chapter 4) and the sending of its first missionaries to Jerusalem in 1851. Following this unsuccessful venture, Africa was chosen as the next field of labor, and Alexander Cross, a Negro, became the first missionary (1854). The missionary endeavor

1. Ruth Isabel Seabury, *So Send I You,* p. 26. Copyright 1955 The Christian Education Press. Used by permission of the United Church Press.

of the American Christian Missionary Society was limited and far from successful. In 1874 the Christian Woman's Board of Missions of the Christian Church (Disciples of Christ) was organized, followed by the organization of the Foreign Christian Missionary Society. Today the Division of Homeland Ministries and the Division of Overseas Ministries carry on much of the work begun by these organizations. The last quarter of the nineteenth century saw the work of overseas witness grow to include work in ten nations outside the United States and Canada.

During the seventy-five years between 1875 and 1950, the missionary movement brought great benefit to many people and at the same time it fell into difficulty because of the rise of nationalism. Since 1945 the missionary movement has made a series of rapid changes which began with a disassociation of missionary work from colonialism and the establishment of a system of "partnerships" with the churches in the new nations. However, nationalism became a power in world affairs and the development of "partnerships" faded.

At the beginning of the 1970s three new factors must be dealt with on the scene of overseas ministry: first, the integrity of the overseas church, which was once a "receiving" church and the object of missionary endeavor; second, the increasing amount of cooperative overseas work among denominations as a result of the ecumenical movement; and, third, receiving the contributions of the overseas churches as full participants in the whole church in the world. For example, funds are requested by the Christian Church (Disciples of Christ) in the Democratic Republic of Congo (Kinshasa) for its support. The Congo church also asks for workers needed because of their special expertise. Such workers generally have short-term assignments and there is little possibility of anyone being assigned to one place for lifetime work.

The overseas ministry of the Christian Church (Disciples of Christ) is related to a united church in Thailand, North India, Japan, and the Philippines. The work in Indonesia is basically ecumenical. In Latin and South America and India, the United Church of Christ and the Christian Church (Disciples of Christ) are working under a combined administrative staff.

The need for overseas ministry is greater than ever. However, it is different from that of seventy-five years ago. Today the work requires increased financial support and the dedicated labors of experts in the fields of education, medicine, construction, agriculture, and sanitation. Building houses and desalinization plants, establishing new systems of education, drilling wells, and planning irrigation projects are but a few of the kinds of work being carried on in this ministry.

With the problems of rising population and developing nationalism in the Third World, the needs of the overseas ministry are greater than ever. There is, also, an increasing need for congregations to discover and respond to the interrelatedness between cultural, economic, and political developments in the United States and Canada and those of other nations. God's mission in the world is pressing upon the individual and the congregation, calling for individual and corporate response.

Outreach at Home

Outreach at home requires knowledge and support of, and involvement in, the work of the general and regional manifestations of the church; home mission institutions; new church establishment and maintenance; recruitment and guidance for the ministry; programs to help minority-ethnic groups and the homeless, orphaned, and aged; the chaplaincy; the development of curriculum and educational program; evangelism and churchmanship; constituency groups such as Christian Women's Fellowship, Christian Men's Fellowship, and youth groups; undergraduate and seminary education; and ministerial relief. Not all of these areas of work will be given attention in this chapter. Those dealt with are done so to indicate the kind of work involved. Detailed information concerning each area of work is found in Appendix A. Outreach at home is primarily designed to serve individuals, institutions, and congregations in the United States and Canada.

Home mission institutions presently a part of the Christian Church (Disciples of Christ) are: Hazel Green Academy, Hazel Green, Kentucky; All Peoples Christian Center, Los Angeles, California; Inman Christian Center, San Antonio, Texas; and Yakima Indian Christian Mission, Toppenish, Washington. The church has a working relationship with Tougaloo College, Tougaloo, Mississippi, and with a migrant work center, Marana, Arizona. Institutional mission work was initiated by the Christian Woman's Board of Missions (one of the organizations that joined in forming The United Christian Missionary Society) as early as 1880.

Outreach work at home has made a substantial contribution in many areas of life of the Christian Church (Disciples of Christ), among which is that of new church establishment and maintenance. This work has had deep roots in the history of the church for more than one hundred years. Literally hundreds of congregations have come into being and been nurtured to maturity through the efforts of the home ministry of the church. The work of new church establishment and maintenance has been complemented by the services of the Board of Church Extension in providing loans—some of them interest free—for purchasing land and for erecting buildings.

Work with minority-ethnic groups, chaplains, and constituency groups in the United States and Canada has long been, and continues to be, an essential part of outreach at home. The nature and magnitude of this work seem often to be dictated by the changing scene in the United States.

Work among minority-ethnic groups began when immigrants flooded into the United States and then settled in certain areas of the country. The church gave special service to Italians, Orientals, French-Acadians, Mexicans, and others. The Christian Church (Disciples of Christ) gave special special attention to the needs of the freedman at the close of the Civil War. In the years following, the American Christian Missionary Society, the Christian Woman's Board of Missions, and The United Christian Missionary Society, all acting in behalf of congregations in the United States and Canada, gave funds and services to Negro congregations and various institutions developed for them. The United Society, through its structures, cooperated with the National Christian Missionary Convention, an organization that served predominantly Negro congregations. The National Christian Missionary Convention recently became the National Convocation of the Christian Church (Disciples of Christ).

For these minority-ethnic groups the church, through the American Society, the Christian Woman's Board of Missions, and the United Society, established educational institutions, social service centers, and churches as a part of its outreach at home.

In recent years the emphasis has changed—rightly and also belatedly so—with the focus on civil and moral rights. The drive for black identity has brought powerful forces to bear on the church to increase its witness not only to black people but to Hispanic people (Mexican, Puerto Rican, Cuban), Indians, Appalachians—all those minority-ethnic groups that have been denied, or have found it difficult to enter, the mainstream of church and national life.

Outreach at home has long conducted its work in an interdenominational and ecumenical style. This is evident in work carried on in cooperation with city, state, and national councils of churches. In addition, such work is currently developed through consortia designed to help denominations work together on projects such as development of an educational program for congregations, new church establishment, inner-city projects, and work with the ministry.

The congregation cannot develop a balanced outreach response to God's mission without substantial efforts at home.

Outreach in Higher Education

Higher education was early a part of the concern of Alexander Campbell. Bacon College was founded by the Christian Church (Disciples of Christ) at Georgetown, Kentucky, in 1836, followed by Bethany College, founded by Alexander Campbell four years later. The church took seriously Campbell's concern for higher education and established hundreds of "academies" (basically high schools), colleges, and universities. At the present time thirty-four colleges, universities, seminaries, and Bible chairs are related to the Board of Higher Education of the Christian Church (Disciples of Christ), three of which are outside the United States.

The congregation benefits from the work of higher education in terms of trained leadership—both clergy and laity—for the work of responding to God's mission in the congregation. It is imperative, therefore, that the congregation have knowledge of, and involvement in, this portion of God's mission and give support to it.

Outreach to the Homeless, Orphaned, and Aged

Outreach ministry and witness to the homeless, orphaned, and aged is a responsibility shared by several areas of work in the Christian Church (Disciples of Christ). The Division of Social and Health Services, long known as the National Benevolent Association, is a well-known part of the work of the church in response to God's mission in the world. It seeks to provide institutional care for children and aged persons in nineteen institutions scattered across the United States. Many people have been served through the work of this organization.

This practical response to the needs of people deserves the knowledge, support, and involvement of the congregations.

Organization in Brief

The congregation, in order to respond to God's mission, will find it helpful to have a committee, department, commission, or task group dealing with outreach. This group would be appointed by the authority of, and would be responsible to, the general board. Its work would be coordinated in the congregation's life by the cabinet.

The group dealing with outreach would be responsible for the following:

- Provide opportunity for the congregation to study the program and needs served by the various kinds of outreach work of the church.
- Involve the various groups in the congregation in supporting the outreach work of the church. Such groups would represent the educational, worship, devotional, and constituency life of the congregation.
- Prepare askings for the congregational budget for all concerns related to outreach. (Many congregations find it helpful to have a percentage increase in this budget authorized by the general board of the congregation. This percentage is 1 to 5 percent above that of inflation per annum.)

Support of the outreach ministry and witness budget of the congregation may be developed along several lines. The congregation should survey its resources for the support of its outreach witness. At present these include special day offerings taken on Easter, Children's Day, Thanksgiving, and Christmas. (The Week of Compassion offering is over and above these. Support of Reconciliation is by individuals through congregations and is over and above all of the preceding.) The Christian Women's Fellowship offerings and the offerings of all youth groups are a part of the congregation's response to these needs and should also be included in a survey of the congregation's resources. The regular congregational offerings received in the form of pledged commitments and loose offerings are another vital part of the resources available.

The congregation will want to establish the percentage of its total budget that it will provide for meeting outreach needs. The goal for the congregation may be 50/50 giving. This is achieved by first determining what percentage is presently being used for outreach support. It may be anywhere from 5 to 25 percent, or more. Whatever it is, the congregation will be able to achieve 50/50 giving by automatically increasing the percent of its budget for outreach witness each year on a progressive schedule. A congregation in the Midwest has followed this practice and has continued to make substantial gains above inflation in support of outreach needs despite the rising cost of its congregational operations and social involvement work.

The congregation is responsible for responding to God's mission in the world. The committee, department, commission, or task group on outreach has no small task. The cry of the poor and the needs of all people must be vivid in their minds and hearts. The result will be individuals and congregations turned outward to the whole world and responding to God's mission.

APPENDIXES

Appendix A

Following is a list of some important sources of information that will be helpful to those wishing to make maximum use of this book:

Organizations of the Christian Church (Disciples of Christ)

- Board of Church Extension, 110 S. Downey Avenue, Indianapolis, Indiana 46219. Information available regarding loans and consultative services to administrative units, institutions, and congregations.
- Board of Higher Education, 222 S. Downey Avenue, Indianapolis, Indiana 46219. Information available regarding the institutions of higher education, including seminaries.
- Christian Board of Publication, Box 179, St. Louis, Missouri 63166. Information available regarding curriculum materials, hymnbooks, church equipment, etc.
- Christian Church Foundation, Box 19107, Indianapolis, Indiana 46219. Information available regarding individual and corporate units of the church investing in the current and future work of the church.
- Council on Christian Unity, 222 S. Downey Avenue, Indian-

apolis, Indiana 46219. Information available concerning ecumenical involvements of the Christian Church (Disciples of Christ), including the Consultation on Church Union (COCU).

- Disciples of Christ Historical Society, 1101 Nineteenth Avenue S., Nashville, Tennessee 37212. Information available regarding historical materials of the church.
- Division of Homeland Ministries, 222 S. Downey Avenue, Indianapolis, Indiana 46219. Information available from various offices of the division on church organizations, the ministry, specific program areas, program-planning, church vocations, research, leader development, curriculum, etc.
- Division of Overseas Ministries, 222 S. Downey Avenue, Indianapolis, Indiana 46219. Information available regarding the work of the church overseas.
- Division of Social and Health Services (National Benevolent Association), 115 N. Jefferson Avenue, St. Louis, Missouri 63103. Information available regarding the homes for the aged and children and other services.
- Pension Fund of Christian Churches (Disciples of Christ), 700 Test Building, Indianapolis, Indiana 46204. Information available regarding ministerial relief, pensions, and Week of the Ministry.
- Regional (State/Area) Organizations ... see the *Year Book and Directory of the Christian Church (Disciples of Christ)*. Information available regarding regional planning, program and promotional concerns.
- Unified Promotion, 222 S. Downey Avenue, Indianapolis, Indiana 46219. Information available concerning special-day offering materials, stewardship materials, and the Week of Compassion.

Current Publications of the Christian Church (Disciples of Christ)

- *Annual Planning Guide and Calendar,* Division of Homeland Ministries, 222 S. Downey Avenue, Indianapolis, Indiana

46219. Order from Christian Board of Publication, Box 179, St. Louis, Missouri 63166.

- *Bethany Guide,* Box 179, St. Louis, Missouri 63166.
- *Christian Board of Publication General Catalog,* Christian Board of Publication, Box 179, St. Louis, Missouri 63166.
- *Christian Church Curriculum Guide,* Department of Christian Education, Division of Homeland Ministries (UCMS), 222 S. Downey Avenue, Indianapolis, Indiana 46219, and Christian Board of Publication, Box 179, St. Louis, Missouri 63166. Order from Christian Board of Publication.
- Church Program Guidance Manuals: *The Congregation Plans for Action, Christian Action and Community Service, Christian Education, Evangelism, Membership, Stewardship and Church Finance, Property, World Outreach, Worship, Christian Men's Fellowship, Christian Women's Fellowship.* Division of Homeland Ministries, 222 S. Downey Avenue, Indianapolis, Indiana 46219. Order from Christian Board of Publication, Box 179, St. Louis, Missouri 63166.
- *Discipliana,* Disciples of Christ Historical Society, 1101 Nineteenth Avenue S., Nashville, Tennessee 37212.
- *Glance,* 222 S. Downey Avenue, Indianapolis, Indiana 46219.
- *Guideposts,* 222 S. Downey Avenue, Indianapolis, Indiana 46219.
- *Mid-Stream,* Council on Christian Unity, 222 S. Downey Avenue, Indianapolis, Indiana 46219.
- *NBA Family Talk,* 115 N. Jefferson Avenue, 2d floor, St. Louis, Missouri 63103.
- *Social Action News Letter,* 222 S. Downey Avenue, Indianapolis, Indiana 46219.
- *Vanguard,* Division of Homeland Ministries, 222 S. Downey Avenue, Indianapolis, Indiana 46219. Subscriptions: Box 179, St. Louis, Missouri 63166.
- *World Call,* 222 S. Downey Avenue, Indianapolis, Indiana

46219. Subscriptions: Box 179, St. Louis, Missouri 63166.

- *Year Book and Directory of the Christian Church (Disciples of Christ)*, General Office of the Christian Church (Disciples of Christ), 222 S. Downey Avenue, Indianapolis, Indiana 46219. Order from Christian Board of Publication, Box 179, St. Louis, Missouri 63166.

Ecumenical or Interdenominational Organizations

- National Council of the Churches of Christ in the U.S.A., 475 Riverside Drive, New York, New York 10027. Information available concerning interdenominational planning and program. Also publishes a newsletter, *Tempo*.
- World Council of Churches, Room 439, 475 Riverside Drive, New York, New York 10027. Information regarding the work of the Council, including overseas ministry.

Appendix B

Planning at the general (national and international), regional (state/area), and congregational levels of the church may be described as follows:

General Level

- Develop and recommend long-range program goals for the church.
- Develop and recommend objectives to make these goals effective.
- Plan program, including goals, objectives, and supporting resources, for use by the regional and congregational manifestations of the church—such program to be related to the priorities established by the church.

- Provide the means of interchange of concerns and ideas among all manifestations of the Christian Church (Disciples of Christ).

Regional Level

- Provide for responsible representation of a general (national and international) planning body.
- Receive and make appropriate use of recommendations for program from the general offices of the church.
- Develop regional long-range goals.
- Develop regional objectives to make these goals effective.
- Recommend program for the region to the appropriate legislative bodies of the region for action.
- Use regional staff to aid in the administration of the approved program for the congregations of the region.

Congregational Level

- Provide for a responsible planning procedure and leaders.
- Receive and make appropriate use of recommendations for program from both the general and regional offices of the church. Program resources are available to congregations from both the general and regional offices of the church. In addition, *Vanguard, Bethany Guide,* and *World Call* provide specific aids in program and supporting resources for congregational use. File folders can be used to keep communications from general and regional offices as well as to keep suggestions from groups and individuals within the congregation concerning program. Such resources should be available to planning groups on a regular basis.
- Establish the congregation's statement of mission (purpose) in response to God's mission in the world, and develop long-range and measurable action targets (objectives) for annual achievement.
- Recommend program for the congregation to the appro-

priate legislative bodies of the congregation for action. Program generally emerges from the congregation's committees, departments, or task groups and is coordinated by the cabinet and legislated by the general board and the congregation. Program should be identified with budget, recognizing that program dictates budget.

- Provide for the laity to work actively with the minister(s) in the administration of the approved program of the congregation. Groups that do the planning of program should be responsible for administering the approved program.

The relatedness and supportiveness of the manifestations of the church to one another can be understood by beginning with what Paul described in the twelfth chapter of 1 Corinthians as the *wholeness* of the church. The church is, therefore, to be understood in its *wholeness* rather than in terms of its separate parts or the sum of its parts. Each manifestation of the church—general, regional, and congregational—has its appropriate work to do in support of the wholeness of the "body of Christ."

It would be relatively easy to identify the task of each manifestation of the church if each stood alone, sufficient within itself. Such, however, is not the case; each manifestation is dependent in one way or another on the others. One thing is imperative: each manifestation must have a view of the wholeness of the church and its responsibility to respond to God's mission in the world. Given this view, each manifestation can work out its appropriate responsibilities in witness. Following are some suggestions of each manifestation's responsibilities:

General (national and international) responsibilities

- Provide organization and administration of national expressions of witness in mission
- Provide for unified planning and programs, projects, events, and supporting materials which may be used by regions and congregations
- Provide for a unified approach to financial support for pro-

grams, projects, events, and administration of witness of all manifestations of the church

- Provide those services which cannot be provided as efficiently by smaller units of the church (for example: curriculum plans and materials, development of concerns of nationwide dimensions and systems of interrelated communication between the units of the church)
- Provide for involvement in and relatedness to ecumenical and secular units of society on a national and international scale
- Provide the creative research and staff expertise necessary for the development of programs, projects, events, and supporting materials useful by both regions and congregations
- Provide the opportunity for the communication of information related to programs, projects, events, and supporting materials to regions and congregations

Regional (state/area) responsibilities

- Provide organization and administration of regional expressions of witness in mission
- Provide for participation in unified planning of programs, projects, events, and supporting materials at the general level of the church
- Provide for regional planning for those programs, projects, events, and supporting materials appropriate to the needs of the region, using the results of general planning as a primary resource
- Provide for participation in a unified approach to financial support at the regional level of the church for the work of all manifestations of the church
- Provide for those services which can be most effectively and efficiently provided by the region (for example: ministerial placement, counseling with ministers and congregations, maintaining vital lines of program communication with

congregations, and providing an important channel of two-way communication between the general and the congregational manifestations of the church)

- Provide for involvement in and relatedness to ecumenical and secular units of society within the region
- Provide for the opportunity for the communication of information related to programs, projects, events, and supporting materials to congregations

Congregational responsibilities

- Provide organization and administration of congregational expressions of witness in mission
- Provide for congregational planning of programs, projects, events, and supporting materials, making use of regional, general, and ecumenical resources
- Provide for congregational participation in district and regional events and programs, and provide for congregational expressions concerning regional and general programs, projects, events, and supporting resources
- Provide for financial support from the congregation for work of various units of the church, including the support of the congregation
- Provide the prophetic, teaching-learning, pastoral, and priestly work of the church to the members of the congregation and of the community
- Provide for involvement in and relatedness to ecumenical and secular units of the community
- Provide for the opportunity for the communication to the congregation of information related to programs, projects, events, and supporting materials

BIBLIOGRAPHY

Bibliography

Anderson, Courtney. *To the Golden Shore: The Life of Adoniram Judson*. Boston: Little, Brown and Company, 1956.

Ayres, Francis O. *The Ministry of the Laity: A Biblical Exposition*. Philadelphia: Westminster Press, 1962.

Bonhoeffer, Dietrich. *The Communion of Saints: A Dogmatic Inquiry into the Sociology of the Church*. Translated by R. Gregor Smith. New York: Harper & Row, 1963.

———. *The Cost of Discipleship*. Translated by R. H. Fuller. Rev. and unabr. ed. New York: Macmillan Co., 1959.

Brunner, Emil. *The Letter to the Romans: A Commentary*. Translated by H. A. Kennedy. Philadelphia: Westminster Press, 1959.

Campbell, Alexander. *The Christian System*. 2d ed. Cincinnati: Central Book Concern, 1839.

Campbell, Alexander, ed. *The Christian Baptist*. 15th ed., rev. by D. S. Burnet from the 2d ed., with Campbell's last corrections. Vol. 1 of 7 vols. (complete in one book). St. Louis: Christian Publishing Co., n.d.

The Church for Others and the Church for the World. Geneva: World Council of Churches, 1968.

Cogley, John. *Religion in a Secular Age.* New York: Frederick A. Praeger, 1968.

Durant, Will. *The Age of Faith.* Story of Civilization, vol. 4. New York: Simon & Schuster, 1950.

Garrison, W. E. *Religion Follows the Frontier: A History of the Disciples of Christ.* New York: Harper & Brothers, 1931.

Glasse, James D. *Profession: Minister.* New York: Abingdon Press, 1968.

Grimes, Howard. *The Rebirth of the Laity.* New York: Abingdon Press, 1962.

Harkness, Georgia. *The Church and Its Laity.* New York: Abingdon Press, 1962.

Humbert, Royal, ed. *A Compend of Alexander Campbell's Theology.* St. Louis: Bethany Press, 1961.

Jud, Gerald J.; Mills, Edgar W., Jr.; and Burch, Genevieve Walters. *Ex-Pastors: Why Men Leave the Parish Ministry.* Philadelphia: United Church Press, 1970.

Küng, Hans. *The Church.* New York: Sheed & Ward, 1967.

Kuntz, Kenneth A. *The Minister and the Christian Life Curriculum.* St. Louis: Christian Board of Publication, 1968.

Lee, Robert, and Galloway, Russell. *The Schizophrenic Church: Conflict over Community Organization.* Philadelphia: Westminster Press, 1969.

Lentz, Richard E. *Solving Leadership Problems.* St. Louis: Christian Board of Publication, n.d.

Lentz, Richard E.; Vieth, Paul H.; and Henthorne, Ray L. *Our Teaching Ministry.* St. Louis: Christian Board of Publication, 1967.

McLuhan, Marshall. *Understanding Media: The Extensions of Man.* New York: McGraw-Hill Book Company, 1964.

Macquarrie, John. *Studies in Christian Existentialism.* Philadelphia: Westminster Press, 1965.

Medearis, Dale W. *The Congregation Plans for Action.* Church Program Guidance Manuals. Indianapolis: National Church Program Coordinating Council, 1966.

Michalson, Carl. *Worldly Theology: The Hermeneutical Focus of an Historical Faith.* New York: Charles Scribner's Sons, 1967.

Millennial Harbinger. 1832, p. 115; 1838, pp. 386, 389; 1845, pp. 108–9, 259; 1848, pp. 377, 382–83; 1851, p. 30; 1862, p. 110.

Neve, Herbert T. *Sources for Change.* Geneva: World Council of Churches, 1968.

Norton, Perry L., ed. *Search.* New York: Division of Home Mission, National Council of the Churches of Christ in the U.S.A., 1960.

A Provisional Design for the Christian Church (Disciples of Christ). Adopted at Kansas City, Missouri, 1968.

Rauschenbusch, Walter. *Christianizing the Social Order.* New York: Macmillan Co., 1912.

Ray, Sherburne L. "Iowa Laymen Serve in Prison." *The Christian,* August 25, 1968, p. 24.

Reitz, Rüdiger. *The Church in Experiment.* New York: Abingdon Press, 1969.

The School and the Democratic Environment. New York: Columbia University Press, 1970.

Seabury, Ruth Isabel. *So Send I You.* Philadelphia: Christian Education Press, 1955.

Smith, Ronald Gregor. *Secular Christianity.* New York: Harper & Row, 1966.

Survey of Service: Disciples of Christ. St. Louis: Christian Board of Publication, 1928.

Thérèse of the Child Jesus, Saint. *Thoughts of the Servant of God.* New York: P. J. Kenedy & Sons, 1915.

Tielhard de Chardin, Pierre. *The Phenomenon of Man.* Translated by Bernard Wall. New York: Harper & Row, Harper Torchbooks, 1961.

Wentz, Frederick K. *The Layman's Role Today.* New York: Abingdon Press, 1963.

Wieman, Henry Nelson, and Horton, Walter Marshall. *The Growth of Religion.* New York: Willett, Clark & Company, 1938.

Wieser, Thomas, ed. *Planning for Mission: Working Papers on the New Quest for Missionary Communities.* New York: U.S. Conference for the World Council of Churches, 1966.